JOEL ZIME[

WIN THE CLAIM GAME

An Insider's Guide to a Successful Home Insurance Claim

WIN THE CLAIM GAME
*An Insider's Guide to a Successful
Insurance Claim*

ISBN   978-1-61961-393-5 *Paperback*
        978-1-61961-394-2 *Ebook*

LIONCREST
PUBLISHING

CONTENTS

Introduction

———

Imagine coming home from a nice evening and finding that your house has burned to the ground. Or that someone has smashed in your front door and cleaned out all of your valuables and your prized possessions.

Everyone buys insurance, and everyone hopes to never use it. But, unfortunately, incidents happen. According to the ABI, insurers make over £80m worth of claims payments—every day.[1]

But the industry has changed. The last 20 years has seen a fundamental shift in the way that insurance is marketed and sold in the UK. Commercial Union, which later became a part of Aviva, used to have a very famous slogan: "We won't make a drama out of a crisis." And effectively what that

———

1 https://www.abi.org.uk/~/media/Files/Documents/Publications/Public/2014/Key%20Facts/ABI%20Key%20Facts%202014.pdf

meant was: "When you have a problem, you can lean on us. Don't worry about it. We'll take care of it." As recent as the mid to late 1990s, you would go to your trusted local broker to buy your home insurance policy. The broker would make recommendations and you would buy based on the level of service you would get and expect at the time of a claim.

That all changed when companies like Direct Line cut out the middleman and started selling directly to the consumer. Now, instead of an expert broker making recommendations and weighing up the pros and cons of different policies, it's the customer who has to do the same. And given that most of us have better things to do than read through 20 different insurance policy wordings, we began to focus on the one thing that we did understand: the price.

Price comparison websites accelerated this shift. Now, when comparethemarket.com or confused.com spit out your quotes, household insurers are competing to be at the top of the list with the lowest price, because—surprise, surprise— that's the one that most people pick, often assuming that all the policies listed are pretty much the same.

The end result is that no one is buying based on level of cover or claims service anymore so there's no incentive for insurance companies to compete in these areas and provide better service and better cover. Add to that, too, the fact that an insurance company's biggest cost is its claims bill. The easiest way to reduce costs and therefore reduce prices is to pay out fewer claims or pay out a smaller amount of money.

One way that insurers reduce their claims bill is to have loss adjusters handle their claims for them. In most instances, what they do is pay a loss adjuster a fixed fee for each claim and then instruct the loss adjuster to act on their behalf to settle that claim under what's known as "delegated authority." Immediately, then, the loss adjuster has an incentive to lower their own costs and work more efficiently, often at the expense of service to the claimant. And the loss adjusters themselves will have their own preferred suppliers—people like builders, repairers, plasterers, and other specialists who do things like dry out your front room if you've had a flood. In fact, they might even have associate companies like these where they claim the fees for the work from the insurer themselves or have a network of suppliers who give them a commission for referring work.

So what does this mean for you as a policyholder? What it means is that if the worst happens and you do have to make an insurance claim, no one else will have your interests at heart. It's up to you to manage your claim.

That's not as easy as it sounds. If you're lucky, you won't have to make many claims in your lifetime. But an insurance company or a loss adjuster deals with thousands every year so, if you do have to make a claim, you're put in a difficult and unfamiliar situation at a time of extreme trauma and you're dealing with seasoned professionals who know exactly how the game is played. This means the cards are stacked against you from the off.

Well, I'm here to give you the inside information you need to level the playing field. I've been dealing with insurance claims since 1987 and started my own company in 1999 to help people successfully manage their claims. I've learnt a trick or two in that time.

In this book, I'll walk you step-by-step through the claims process, from the moment you suffer a loss to the day your life is back on track again. You'll know exactly what to do at every stage and you'll be in a good position to get the outcome you want.

Let's get started.

CHAPTER ONE

The Mindset for Dealing with Insurance Companies

———

I wish no one ever had to read this book. If nothing bad ever happened to you, then you'd never need to make an insurance claim and you'd never need my advice. The world would be a better place and this book would sell zero copies, but everyone would be happy.

Unfortunately, life isn't like that. If you're making an insurance claim, it means that something has happened to you that you would have preferred not to happen: a burst pipe, a fire, a flood, a burglary, whatever the incident may be. Something has happened that has caused you a loss, large or small. That's life and it happens. That's what insurance is for. And when that loss has happened, you've decided, "Okay, I can't take this on the chin myself. I'll call the insurance company."

This is often at a time of deep distress, especially if you've suffered a particularly bad loss. And you're about to get through to an automated line that asks you to "Press 1 for flood claims, press 2 for burglary claims, press 3 for fire claims" and then puts you on hold for an hour with some cheesy, relaxed music. Your problems seem insurmountable and you just want someone to listen to you and help you out. But you've heard all the horror stories in the media or from your mates at the pub. Everyone has a tale to tell about how they got screwed over by greedy insurance companies who refuse to pay out. You're not going to let that happen to you.

Your mind-set at that moment is crucial. If you make that call to your insurer believing that you'll have to fight them tooth and nail every step of the way, then you've already lost. You've adopted the wrong mind-set, believing that the insurance company is the enemy and that you have to "beat" them and "win" the claim. Treating the insurer as the enemy means that you'll be focusing on all the wrong things. Every time your insurer asks you a question, you'll be thinking, "Why do they want to know that? Why is that relevant?" and wondering if you gave the right answer or not. You'll be caught up in the details of the process.

This is wrong. Do not think of the insurance company as the enemy.

All that does is move you further away from your goal, and your goal should be to have your claim settled swiftly, easily, to your satisfaction, and in the manner of your choosing so that you can recover from the loss you've suffered and get on with your life.

THE RIGHT MINDSET TO ADOPT

The reality is that the insurance company is not the enemy. They are set up to pay you—and want to pay you. If they consistently refused to pay out legitimate claims, they'd soon be out of business. The whole reason that an insurance company exists is to take in money in the form of premiums and pay it out to you when you need it. In fact, few insurers actually make money from the insurance side of their business. Their profit actually comes from the fact that between you paying money in premiums and receiving money in claims payouts, the insurer gets to hold onto the money and invest it.

But the insurance company is dealing with its own problems. It wants to pay out claims—but only legitimate claims. They don't want to hand out money to fraudsters. Every pound that gets paid out to fraudsters is an extra pound that either can't be paid out to a legitimate claimant or has to be paid in premium by an honest person. In fact, the ABI estimates that fraud costs every policyholder an extra £50 in premiums every year.[2] Not only that, but the insurance company wants to pay out the right amount to settle your claim—but no more than that. Paying out more than is necessary is known in the industry as "leakage" and no one wants to see their money go to dishonest people like that.

You might be familiar with the case of Lord Brocket, an upstanding old Etonian, former Army Lieutenant, and land-owning Baron. He had a fantastic collection of classic

---

2   https://www.abi.org.uk/Insurance-and-savings/Topics-and-issues/Fraud

cars until two of them went missing one day. He claimed for them, as you would do if they were stolen, and pocketed the money. The two "stolen" cars were later found buried in his back garden, and Lord Brocket was sentenced to five years for insurance fraud. That's an extreme example, but insurers are filtering for dishonest people like that, or even people who will just stretch the truth, exaggerate, try and get an extra couple of hundred pounds here or there. It's all money out of their pocket, so they're filtering for reasons *not* to pay rather than reasons *to* pay. They might even use lie detectors on the phone to try and pick out the dishonest from the genuine claimants.

And think about it from the insurer's point of view. They don't know that you're a trustworthy and reliable person. They haven't spent enough time with you to get to know you as an individual. To the insurer (or, more usually, their loss adjuster), you're just a policy number and a claim number that they have to deal with. Insurers deal with hundreds of claims every day, and to do that, they have to have processes in place to deal with them consistently and systematically. If that means that they have to ask you to fill out a bunch of forms, then that's what you have to do, and you won't gain anything by fighting them.

So get out of the battle mind-set. Remember: this is not a battle, you're not trying to win, and the insurance company is not the enemy.

Instead, adopt the mind-set: this is my claim to make, not the insurance company's claim to dictate.

That's why you bought this book. You want to take ownership of the situation and be in control of the outcome of your claim.

This goes right down to every detail of the claim. If you've had a computer game stolen and the insurer offers you £10 for it, but you know damn well that it would cost £20 to replace and can prove that, then you're well within your rights to ask for the £20. This isn't battling the insurer; rather, it's taking control of the process. You might have to work within the insurer's processes and procedures in order to progress your claim, but that's fine. All you need to do is to give the insurer the information they need so the insurer can give you what you want. This first means deciding what it is you actually want from the insurer.

SET YOUR GOALS

This is your claim to make, not the insurance company's to dictate. So you need to decide: What do I want out of this? What is my end goal? How do I want to receive the settlement?

All insurance policies are based upon the idea of indemnity: that you should be put back in the same position you were before you suffered a loss. That sounds pretty simple but there are actually a few different ways of doing that. In fact, there are four main options for settlement of a claim:

1. REPAIR OR REINSTATE

The insurer—or their subcontractor—repairs the item that was damaged. Only possible if the item is repairable. If not, the insurer may class it as "beyond economic repair" and elect to replace the item instead.

2. REPLACE

The insurer will replace the item for you. This may be on a *new-for-old* basis, where you receive a brand new version of the item, or a *like-for-like* basis, where you receive an item of similar age and quality as yours.

3. DIMINUTION IN MARKET VALUE

The insurer will pay you an amount commensurate with the loss in value of an item. This mainly applies to buildings claims where your house has been damaged and, for whatever reason, can't be repaired. The insurer will pay you an amount equal to the decrease in market value of your house.

4. CASH

Simple: whatever the insurer would spend to settle your claim themselves, they'll give you in cash.

These aren't exclusive options. If you have a lot of items destroyed, you may choose to settle some by way of repair, some will be replaced, and you'll take cash for others. These are the insurer's options to exercise, rather than yours, but in general, insurers are looking to settle at the cheapest of all options. That said, they'll often listen to your requests as part of the FCA's *Treating Customers Fairly* initiative. You should decide what basis of settlement is best for you, based on what you're trying to achieve.

Here's an example. If my client's house burned down, he'd still need somewhere to live, so naturally he would ask the insurer to restore his home to its earlier condition rather than take a large cash settlement. But let's instead imagine a different scenario: a small kitchen fire that damages some of the tiles and units in your kitchen, doing around £5,000 worth of damage.

You could choose to get that damage fixed and your kitchen repaired to what it was before. But what if you've been saving up to get your kitchen completely redone? It's not worth the hassle to have it repaired by the insurer, only for you to come in and replace everything later on. In that instance, you'd be better off asking for a cash settlement and then using that cash towards your kitchen remodelling fund and, as part of that work, fixing any damage caused by the fire.

Neither path is right or wrong. But to decide what you'd be happiest with, you need to understand your needs and wants and build your claim around those. I'll say it again: this is your claim to make, not the insurance company's to dictate.

Another example: a different client of mine had some lovely curtains that were damaged during a heavy flood. The insurance company appointed a restoration company to clean, repair, and rehang them. She called us, distraught, and said, "These curtains are ruined!" We went round and looked at them, these nice orange curtains, and we all thought they looked fine. We asked her what the problem was. She said, "They used to be blue." The chemicals that the cleaners had used had taken all the colour out of them.

It's an extreme example but it illustrates that you have to be the arbiter of the outcome of the claim; otherwise, it'll be the process that determines the outcome and not you as the customer. If you're not happy with the way that things are being done, you should absolutely stand up and say so to the insurer. If you defer those decisions to the insurer, you're in trouble. You need to take ownership.

ASSESS THE TERRAIN

To take ownership, you need to understand the situation you're in. The only way you can control the process is first to understand the process. As I said before, insurance companies are trying to keep their costs down and don't want to pay out more than they need to in order to settle a claim. So to minimise the chances of that happening, they've put in place a bunch of different processes, standard operating procedures, forms, and the like intended to standardise the entire end-to-end claims process. You have to understand and work within all of the insurance company's processes in order to effectively take control of your claim. This may seem awkward and annoying but think of it as taking a short detour on your way to where you want to go.

Here's an example of understanding the process. A client of mine suffered some water damage recently and needed a lot of building work done to restore his house. He got a quote for the work from a local builder whom he knows and trusts, which came out at £45,000. The insurance company did their own assessment and said the work would actually only cost £30,000. They offered my client a cash settlement for that amount. So he's out £15,000, right? Wrong.

A cash settlement isn't the only option in this case. He can also ask the insurance company to appoint their own builders and carry out the work themselves. And once they agree to carry out the work and reinstate my client's home to its previous condition, they're on the hook for the entirety of the job regardless of the final cost. In fact, even if the total costs end up exceeding the policy limits, it doesn't matter, because at that point the insurance company has said they'll do the work at their cost, so they have to keep their word. If the insurer "elects" to reinstate you, they're on the hook to do just that.

Another example: say your grandmother's wedding ring has been stolen. It's a nice ring, worth £5,000, but you mainly kept it for sentimental value. The insurance company can offer to replace it with a similar ring of equivalent value, but you might want to go to Hawaii on holiday in memory of Gran instead, so you elect to take the cash this time. Just a note: the ring might have a retail value of £5,000, but the insurer could replace that at a discount—say, £3,500—so it's the lesser of those two figures that you'll receive, subject to their ability to replace the item.

UTMOST GOOD FAITH

There's an old insurance principle called "utmost good faith" that you should be aware of, too. Bear with me here—I won't get too technical.

Normally, when you buy goods or services, you're buying them under the principle of *caveat emptor*, which means "buyer beware." We've all heard that phrase before. It means that if whatever you bought turns out to be duff goods, well, that's your fault for buying them. When you're buying a second-hand car, the person selling isn't obligated to tell you everything that's wrong with the car, its entire history, or whether it's ever been in an accident—even if you ask the seller outright.

Insurance isn't like that. Insurance operates under the principle of *utmost good faith*. What that means is that you're obligated to be entirely honest and open with the insurer if they ask you a question. So when it comes to insuring your house and the insurer asks you if you've ever had to make a claim, you can't lie and say no. If you do, and the worst happens and you have to make a claim, then if the insurer finds out that you lied up front, they don't have to pay out your claim. In fact, the whole policy is voided. And when you go to find insurance elsewhere, they'll ask you if any other insurer has ever voided a policy of yours, and this time, you'll have to say yes.

The flipside of that is that the Financial Conduct Authority, which regulates insurance firms, says that the insurer can only refuse to pay your claim if they can prove that you either lied, committed fraud, or materially breached the policy conditions. That's not easy. So instead, when insurance companies suspect fraud, they'll often infer it to the person making the claim. Or they'll take their time or try and frustrate the claimant until the claimant gives in and withdraws the claim.

This is important because it means you need to double check all the information that you gave to the insurance company when you took out the policy. Is any of it incorrect? Has any of it changed?

If you've given incorrect information to the insurer, fix it as soon as you realise. Just call them up, tell them that you made a mistake, and give them accurate information. If it becomes apparent during the course of the claim that you've made a mistake, it's best to be upfront and honest about it. In cases where your mistake is regarded as "innocent", i.e. it was not a deliberate effort to get a cheaper premium or to get the insurer to insure that which they otherwise would not, the financial ombudsman should back you up anyway and force the insurer to pay the claim.

CHAPTER 1 RECAP

- **The insurer is not the enemy.**
- **You have to work within the insurer's processes and procedures to get the outcome that you want.**
- **Set your goals at the outset and decide what exactly you want from the insurer, then work towards those goals.**
- **This is your claim to make, not the insurer's to dictate.**

CHAPTER TWO

Prioritise

———

I'm going to give you a checklist of what to do as soon as you suffer a loss. It doesn't matter whether it's a fire, a flood, a burglary, a burst pipe, or a plane's just hit the side of your house. The steps are the same. They may seem like common sense once you've read them, but I've learnt that common sense isn't so common, especially in the aftermath of a loss. It's a time of distress and it can be difficult to think clearly and logically. Thankfully, you don't have to anymore—you just need to follow these steps.

This checklist contains many general principles that will apply in almost all situations, but there are some specific steps you should take in certain situations, which I've included later.

STEP 1: PRIORITISE

On day one, as soon as you realise that you've suffered a loss, the first step is to work out your priorities. This is your home we're talking about.

Top of the list is deciding whether or not you can still stay in your home. That should be a fairly simple decision to make based on the extent of the damage. If it's serious and you can't stay there any longer, then your first action should be to find alternative accommodation. You need somewhere to be safe, warm, dry, and secure before you start thinking about everything else. This could mean staying with friends or family or booking a hotel for a few nights. That's the first thing you need to do. If you have pets, you also need to make sure that they can either come with you or that you can find somewhere for them to stay in the short-term. There are also agencies that insurers use which are specifically set up to facilitate this, especially in situations where you might be short of cash. If that's the case, phone your insurer.

Once you've found somewhere to sleep that night, you need to mitigate the loss you've suffered. You have to take action to minimise the potential claim. So, for example, if your ground floor is flooded, move as much unaffected stuff as you can upstairs and out of harm's way.

At this point, you should aim to act as though you were uninsured. What that means in practice is that if you need to spend any money to minimise the potential claim, you should only spend money in a reasonable and necessary way. If you do that, then all of those costs should be recoverable but may need to be justified after the event.

It is important to make sure your home is secure. There are

some horrible people out there who know that if something serious happens, people often have to leave their homes unoccupied for a length of time—which your home will be if you've had to find somewhere else to stay—and they'll take advantage of that either by taking what's there or by living in your home and doing more damage during their stay. So secure your home and, if you're staying elsewhere, take any valuables with you as well as things that you cherish, like family photos, or that are irreplaceable, like bank records, birth certificates, etc.

In fact, one thing you can do to prepare for the unpredictable is put together a ready bag. A ready bag is just a small, hand- luggage-sized bag or suitcase that contains everything you'll need if you have to leave your home in a hurry. If the floods of the past few years are anything to go by, when the serious weather hits you need to be able to get out of your house very quickly. This is also true for fires: you never know when a fire is going to break out, but when it does, you have to be ready to evacuate, and so having a ready bag will be a huge help if that ever happens. Another possible solution is to make copies of all your important information and documents and leave them with family or scan them and save them in a cloud-based service like Dropbox or Evernote so that they are accessible from anywhere.

When you and your family are safe and secure in another location, you should take a minute to pause and regroup before diving into the claims process. You need to take some time to think about what is important in this moment— whether that's family, friends, pets, possessions—and make sure that they are safe and protected so that you don't have to worry about them while you go through the claims process. Understand that it could be months until you are back in your home again, depending on the extent of the damage, and you're going to be dealing with this for a while. Now is when you try to get into the mind-set that I talked about: you want to work with the insurance company to get the outcome that you want.

STEP 2: MAKE THE CALL TO THE INSURER

You should call your insurer as soon as is practical after the event has happened. Like I said, you're going to be dealing with this for a while, so as soon as you're in the right mind-set, you might as well get the ball rolling. This should be within 24 hours of the event, if not sooner.

The reason you do that is because while staying with your friends might be nice for a day or two, if they're young, free, and single and you have a family, or they like a quiet house and you've brought your Chihuahua with you, sooner or later they'll start to get annoyed (and rightly so). And hotels are soulless places—fine for a two-day business trip but you don't want to live there for weeks on end. As the reality of your circumstances sinks in, it's natural to get stressed. You don't know when you'll be able to move back home. It's a distressing time and can exacerbate tensions that naturally exist among families. The last thing you want to do is get into a fight or start pointing the finger of blame at people, which you may be prone to do at this time. So you need to call the insurer and they'll find you some reasonable alternative accommodation for the short- and medium-term. It's usually a house or flat that should be comparable to your own home, which the insurer will rent out for you.

A quick note on this: your insurance company in most instances will deem your property to be uninhabitable if you've got no heating, no washing or cooking facilities, or if it's unsafe. If you have all those things, your insurer may declare your property to be habitable anyway. Just because it's unpleasant doesn't mean it's uninhabitable and therefore the costs you incur may not be recoverable.

You'll want to move particularly quickly on this if there's a flood or similar. If all your neighbours have had to move out as well, they might quickly take up all the available housing in the area, so you need to get your claim in fast.

Just note that not all policies provide the same level of cover for accommodation. There will be a financial limit under the policy (possibly a percentage of the sums insured) and a time limit, i.e. the maximum period for which insurers will fund accommodation. Not all accommodation costs will come under this heading. For example, if your furniture needs to go into storage while repair works are being carried out, that could fall under the cost of repairing, not accommodation, i.e. the building policy.

One more thing to note: your insurer will pay a deposit to your temporary landlord, just like in a normal tenancy, to protect that landlord against any damage to the property that you cause while you're staying there. In a normal tenancy situation, you'd get that back at the end of the tenancy, but in this case, the insurer will regard it as a payment to you on your account and deduct it from any final settlement award.

Just something to be aware of.

Again, this is about making yourself and your family safe and secure again and making sure that you have somewhere to live over the next few months while you deal with what's happened. At this point, the fundamentals of the claim are not as important as making yourself and your family secure moving forward.

SPECIFIC SITUATIONS

Like I said, the steps above will take care of the biggest issue you'll be facing at day one and are a good general guide. But there are certain things you need to do in specific situations which depend on what exactly has happened to you. Let's go through them now.

SITUATION #1: BURGLARY

The first thing you'll notice when you come home will be that you can't get into your home, your front door has been destroyed, or, when you get into the house, there's a draft because wind is blowing through a door or window that someone has gone through. The damage will be predominantly to the property, at point of entry. It's very rare these days for people to break into your house and trash the place. That leaves too much evidence, particularly fingerprints and DNA evidence, for the police to find. If you've gotten into a big disagreement with someone it might happen but, generally speaking, if someone's breaking into your house to steal the prized family jewels, they don't want to graffiti the walls and destroy the sofa, too. From the thief's point of view, it's bad for their business—the more evidence they leave, the more likely they are to be caught.

At this point, once you realise that you've been burgled, the first step is to call 999. Don't touch anything; wait for the police to arrive on the scene. While this is happening, you can start on step one above—making sure that your home is secure. In a burglary situation, it's unlikely that you'll need to find alternative accommodation, although, if you have young children, you might want to have them stay with friends or family for the night as the trauma of a burglary can be difficult to understand at a young age.

Securing your home is particularly important given the emotional impact of a burglary. It's very common to feel violated, to feel like your privacy has been invaded, when you've been burgled. So you need to make sure that you can be somewhere where you feel safe.

One of the first things you'll probably want to do is change all your locks and install an alarm system. Most people do this once they've been burgled to get a sense of security. That's fine. Just a word of warning: if you get an alarm, always get one that is certified by the National Security Inspectorate (NSI) or the Security Systems and Alarms Inspection Board (SSAIB). NSI and SSAIB are the two industry-standard regulators that are recognised by insurance companies, and they'll make sure that you're buying a quality system.

If you're getting an alarm system, do it for your own benefit. Do not do it just to get a reduction in your premium. To get a discount on your premium, your insurer will insert a warranty into your policy that will essentially say that they won't pay out in the event of a burglary if your alarm system wasn't operating. And sure as anything, the day you forget or the alarm isn't working, you'll get burgled, and now you've given your insurer a reason not to pay, so you're on your own.

When the police show up, they'll do a search of the house to look around and see what's happened. Then they'll ask you what you think has gone missing. The reason they do that is because they want to be able to convict the thieves in court, and to do that they either need to find forensic evidence that ties the thieves to your house or find your property in the thieves' possession. So the police are immediately looking for what's gone missing, which they'll record as part of their notes on the scene.

The same sorts of items tend to go missing in burglaries— jewellery, cash, and other similar high-risk items—so the police will expect that and ask you for details of items that are easily identifiable as missing. In the next 24 hours or so, you'll get the forensics officer who will show up so, again, don't clean up or tidy up too much before this happens because you don't want to contaminate the scene.

There's a lot of uncertainty and stress in the first 24 hours. The police may have arranged to board up your home or, if not, you need to call your insurance company's emergency help-line and ask them to do it for you. But what happens when you ring your insurer is that they will encourage you, as soon as practicably possible, to detail what's gone missing. At this stage, you haven't really had a chance to gather your thoughts, come to terms with what's happened, and tidy up the house, so you might not know for sure exactly what's gone missing.

LIST OF KEY FRAUD INDICATORS

Here's a sample list of key fraud indicators that insurers may use:

- Adverse claims history
- Claim within six months of starting the policy or very close to renewal, lapse, or cancellation
- Late notification of loss
- Concerns over too little, too much, or altered documentation
- Financial difficulties, court judgements, or default on paying premium
- Failure of security equipment or alarm
- Vague or aggressive attitude or demeanour, lack of cooperation from policyholder
- Large amount of cash or jewellery
- Loss includes very old/out-of-date or very recently purchased items
- No or inadequate proof of ownership or excessive proof of ownership
- Inconsistent story or questions over circumstances of claim
- Any concerns over size of claim/exaggeration
- Policyholder's loss seems inconsistent with lifestyle
- Suspected misrepresentation/non-disclosure of claims issues
- Tip-off from informant/police/HMRC/FCA/FOS

Be aware that if you tick too many of these boxes, your insurer will probably take a closer look at your claim. Not to say that they'll reject it, of course, just that they'll want to take a little more time and care.

The insurance company will require this information from you as soon as possible for a number of reasons, the biggest of which is so that they know whether or not they should look at your claim more closely. Insurers will have a checklist of what they call KFIs, key fraud indicators, and they'll be interested in your list of missing items. High amounts of cash or valuable items can often trigger increased interest in your claim, especially if it seems inconsistent with your lifestyle. In fact, some insurers will use stress test analysers, as I briefly mentioned earlier, when you're on the phone with them—similar to a lie detector—as another potential indicator of fraud. In time, your insurer will expect you to furnish the police with a full and comprehensive list of what's gone missing, which they'll later compare to the list that you've submitted as part of your claim, and compare the two.

Here's a story to show this. One of my clients ended up having to go to the ombudsman over this, and thankfully was successful in his claim. He'd had a large collection of watches stolen, but the initial list that he gave to the police and the insurer on day one was not consistent with the final loss list that was presented to the police and insurers a couple of weeks later, once my client had had the chance to go through and identify everything that was missing. The insurer found this suspicious and initially refused to pay the claim. When we went to the ombudsman, they found in favour of my client, made the insurer pay up, and actually said that they were relieved that the two lists didn't match up because that would be even more suspicious!

What this illustrates is that the insurer has set systems, policies, and procedures in place, and they are filtering for reasons not to pay the claim. Although the majority of people are honest, the procedures are put in place to catch out the bad guys. So don't call the insurance company when you're distressed. You'll go through a bunch of questions to confirm that you are who you say you are, for data protection purposes, which is always annoying and probably won't have anything to do with why you're calling. And if that gets you hot and bothered and stressed, then you're more likely to get picked up by these stress test analysers that insurers use, and so they might be more likely to investigate your claim. That's not what you want at all.

Instead, make sure you're fully prepared. You've checked your policy and you know the details, the conditions, the warranties, the limits, and so on. Then when you're ready, sit down with a nice cup of tea in a nice, composed place and make the call. And when you're on the phone, be very clear with the insurer that, at this juncture, you haven't had the chance to go through and identify everything that's gone missing.

Remember, the point of an insurance policy is to get you back into the position you were in before the loss happened. So at this point, don't think, *You know what? I'll just say my TV's been nicked, too, and get an extra £1,000 from the insurer.* For starters, that's not what many thieves do these days. Widescreen TVs are big, hard to carry, and hard to resell. So if you tag that onto your insurance claim, it will raise red flags, and you're putting yourself at risk of having your whole claim thrown out. It's just not worth it. Of course if an item genuinely has been stolen, don't let the fear of having a lack of credibility deter you from claiming for it.

Give yourself the opportunity to take the time and detail everything that's missing. On the first call, be very explicit and spell out to the insurer that the information you're giving them is just an initial list and that you'll get back to them in a couple of weeks with a full list. If something expensive or important is missing, like your grandmother's ring, definitely mention it in the call—as they'd expect you to notice things like that right away—but don't limit the number of items that have gone missing in that initial phone call. This is very important.

The reason you don't want to cap the number or value of missing items is because you'll end up remembering other items days, weeks, and months later, things that you'd put in drawers and completely forgotten about. If you look at a photograph of yourself from the 1980s, then at first you'll think, *God, I used to wear a lot of Lycra.* But that will start reminding you about what life was like back then, which will remind you of the things that you owned and used at the time, because you're using the photo as a souvenir of that time in your life. That's why Facebook is great. You can go back through all your old photos, in chronological order, and look at what you were wearing and what was around the house, and it will remind you of your life at certain time periods. One other thing you can do is go back over old credit card statements, receipts, anything like that. Large purchases will stand out. You'll look at a credit card statement and think, *Why did I spend £4,000 at that jeweller? Oh right, that ring I bought.*

This serves two purposes. Firstly, this acts as an *aide-mémoire* (something that aids your memory and helps you remember) and will remind you of a lot of things that you'd forgotten about. Secondly, you can use these photos and credit card statements to help to evidence to the insurance company that you owned these items or the items were in your possession at some point. It's not definitive evidence that you owned it—your friend could have loaned you a Cartier watch just for a picture, for example—but it helps to support your claim.

Speaking of evidence of ownership, my clients will often say to me, "My mate's a jeweller, so he can get me a receipt for that." Don't do it. It's not necessary. Firstly, insurers know and understand that you won't have receipts for every single item that you've ever owned. That's just the way it is. Secondly, there are always other ways and means of determining ownership or getting proof of purchase. You don't need to get fake receipts made. All that does is put your whole claim in jeopardy.

One thing you'll also want to think about is talking to Victim Support over the coming days and weeks as well, just to get a sense of security. When someone breaks into your home, they're invading your private space, and it's natural to take it personally. If you feel like you want to talk to someone about it, that's completely normal, and you should do just that.

So, to recap, the specifics for burglary claims:

1. Don't touch anything. Call the police immediately.

2. Wait until you're in a calmer state of mind to call your insurance company and get yourself to a peaceful location to make the call.

3. Take your time during that call and make it clear to the insurer that you don't yet know everything that's gone missing.

4. Over the next couple of weeks, go back through old photographs, bank statements, receipts, and other aide-mémoires to try to put together a more complete list.

5. Don't feel the need to get receipts for everything. The insurer understands that most people don't keep every single receipt.

6. Don't try it on with the insurer. It's not worth the risk.

7. Talk to Victim Support if you feel the need.

SITUATION #2: FIRE

First off, I hope you called the fire brigade. Obviously they'll do what they can to fight and contain the fire and, thanks to their great work, it's rare these days that a fire burns a whole house down. What's more common is that one or two rooms of your house will be severely damaged.

In that scenario, you should start off by taking the steps mentioned earlier in this chapter. First, find alternative accommodation as a matter of urgency, then make the call to your insurer. If you're in rented accommodation, you'll also want to call your landlord or property management company as soon as you possibly can.

Once you've done that—which you should do while still at your house—talk to the fire brigade and ask if and when your home will be safe to re-enter. It might not be for a while because it's totally possible that the fire has caused serious damage to the structural integrity of your house. The fire brigade will be able to tell you what to do.

SITUATION #3: IMPACT OR STORM DAMAGE

Here's another (thankfully rare) situation that needs to be handled differently. If your house has been hit by a large tree or a lorry or a bus, then your house could have major structural damage. At this point, you need to call your insurer's emergency helpline immediately and tell them what's happened as well as inform the emergency services or local authority, who will send a building control officer down to shore up your building, depending on the degree of damage. They'll need to give the building greater protection so that it doesn't collapse.

What this means is that you won't be able to stay in the property, so what you need, just like in the case of fire and flood, is to find alternative accommodation, make your home safe and secure (if you call the insurer's emergency helpline, they'll assist you in making the property secure), and remove any valuables or sentimental items.

This is similar to storm damage, where your roof has blown off or a tree has fallen onto your house. If that's happened, your home is uninhabitable and you'll need to stay somewhere else. You'll still need to get hold of your insurer and they'll arrange some emergency contractors to assist you. If they're overwhelmed because of the surge in business at that time, they will give you authority to either contact their local contractor or appoint your own. In the latter case, you should follow the principle I mentioned earlier: act as though you weren't insured at all. Assuming that you'll bear all the costs is a good way to make sure you only spend what is reasonable and so anything you do spend will be easily justifiable to your insurer later down the line.

One thing to remember with storm damage is that there's no uniform definition of what constitutes a "storm." I know that sounds odd but different insurers will have different definitions, usually dictated by the prevailing wind speed at the time. To you and I, a storm is a storm, but check your policy wording to see exactly how your insurer defines it.

SITUATION #4: ESCAPE OF WATER

In escape of water claims, there's typically a burst pipe or a leak from your plumbing system that's causing water to leak out and damage your property. The first thing in that situation is to stop the leak and mitigate the damage. Turn off your stopcock—it's probably under the sink in your kitchen. Then call a plumber in as soon as possible.

If the leak is on the first or second floor of your house, there's probably some damage to the ceiling, too, and bits of the ceiling might even have come down. Get everything out of the way and out from underneath that bit of ceiling, and then take the ceiling down yourself so that there's no further damage caused.

Aside from that, just get as much as possible out of the path of the water. It seems obvious—and it is—so make sure you do it. These are simple steps you can take to mitigate your loss.

Then call the insurer as soon as you can. They'll get a restoration team out, typically within 24 hours.

One thing to take care of regarding escape of water claims is trace and access. This refers to damage done in the process of discovering and gaining access to repair pipework causing a water leak. Most policies carry a limit of £5,000 for trace and access damage and repairing the damage done.

So if you have a leak, and you think you know where it is, don't do anything. Call the insurer first and inform them of the situation. Say you have to rip up some flooring to get to the leak. Some insurers will only pay to repair those tiles if you phoned them first to get their consent. This is one area where you need to check your policy very carefully. But remember: if you can demonstrate that the areas you need to damage to get to the source of the leak were already damaged by water, then they'll be covered by the water damage limit on your policy, and not the trace and access limit. Photos are useful here.

SITUATION #5: SUBSIDENCE, HEAVE, OR LANDSLIP

Subsidence, heave, and landslip are three similar but slightly different scenarios. Subsidence is when the foundation of the building fails to give the support it needs to, meaning the building moves and is damaged as a result. Heave is the opposite: the ground pushes upwards, damaging the building. Landslip, as it sounds, is where the land under your house moves and is no longer where it started. Who knew that land could do that?

All three have the same end result: the structural integrity of your home is compromised.

This part of the policy always carries a large excess (you are your own insurer for this first sum), usually £1,000-2,500, for which you are liable to the insurer come what may.

The insurer will naturally want to find out what's actually causing the building to move, then determine whether or not that cause can be eliminated and, if it can, later repair the building itself. If the building can't be stabilised or the cause of the movement can't be eliminated, then more serious works like underpinning might be necessary. All of this is complex, specialist work.

If you call up your insurance company and tell them that your house has cracks in the walls, they'll first send their loss adjuster, who in turn will send their surveyors or bring in their structural engineers, frequently in agreement with the insurance company. The loss adjuster will manage the structural engineers, most of whom are either owned or contracted directly to the insurer or loss adjuster. Their advice may not necessarily be impartial or in your best interest, then, so you can't necessarily rely on the efficacy and competency of those engineers or surveyors.

If you have any doubt about these engineers, it's up to you to have them dis-instructed because they are already effectively instructed on your behalf and being paid for by your policy. So you have to demonstrate that what they are proposing is inadequate or inappropriate to your circumstances. And to do that, you need to engage with your own surveyor or structural engineer in order to get a second opinion.

A second opinion at this juncture can cost a good amount of money, on top of the large excess for which you're already liable. If your own engineer comes back and gives the okay to what the insurer's engineers were proposing, you can't recover the money you've spent on your own engineer. You're out of pocket for that, although you will have peace of mind.

So what I would recommend is this: if you see cracks in your property (and they're not always caused by subsidence), you should engage your own structural engineer to begin with and get their view and opinion before you ever talk to the insurance company.

Then, with these reports, go to the insurer and advise them that you've already engaged your own engineer, as you're entitled to do. What this means is that if you do have to make a subsidence claim, you'll still have to pay the excess, but your engineer's fees should be met by the policy and you've got a contractual relationship with that engineer to ensure that all his findings and recommendations are suitable for your situation. The insurer will then take over, manage the whole process, and verify and validate that all the required work has been done.

CHAPTER 2 RECAP

- **Prioritise. Get yourself and your family safe, warm, and dry, either in your own home or in alternative accommodation.**
- **Phone your insurance company. Explain what has happened and be clear that you don't yet know the full extent of the damage.**

- In case of burglary, fire, escape of water, storm damage, or subsidence, there are very particular things that you should be looking out for at the start of the claims process. Look into those carefully.

CHAPTER THREE

Get on Comfortable Ground

When you're dealing with insurance companies, you want to do it on your own terms. Remember, this is your claim to make, not the insurance company's to dictate.

To be on solid ground here, I think you need to know what you're talking about. You need to know the rules of the game. Would you play any sport or game where you didn't know the rules? And even if you did, do you think you'd as well as you could have done if you did actually know the rules? So here's what you need to know to get started.

You need to understand what the insurance company's rights are but, more importantly, what your rights are. Take some time to read your policy. You should look at the policy schedule, look at the coverage you have for contents and buildings, and look at whether or not that includes accidental damage.

Check any endorsements or warranties that may have been imposed upon your policy. That will include single item limits; overall limits to valuables; and limits for accommodation, both in terms of financial or time limits. For example, some policies only cover you for 12 months for alternative accommodation, so just be aware of that.

Look at the policy itself and look at the definitions of your cover. If you've got, for example, a ride-on lawn mower, that might not be covered as part of your content because it could be regarded as a motor vehicle and, therefore, not insured. Sometimes satellite navigation systems are not covered as they are deemed to be an accessory of a motor vehicle and therefore should be insured under your motor policy. You need to be certain on the definitions, particularly for valuables or high-risk items.

Also, be very clear on the basis of settlements so that you know what your rights are and what the insurance company's options are.

As mentioned earlier, the common settlement options are:

- Repair or restore
- Replace (new-for-old or like-for-like)
- Reinstate
- Cash

If you know the insurance company wants to proceed on the basis of replacement, you want to be certain that replacement takes place on your terms or that you exercise your right to request a cash settlement instead. If you are going for replacement or restoration, you need to decide whether or not you want the insurance company's builders to do the work or not. If it's a subsidence claim like we talked about in the last chapter, be clear that you would want to engage with your own surveyor.

Another common clause you should understand is the matching clause. You might have a lovely carpet that matches through your entire home, but only two of the rooms have been damaged. There may well be a clause in your policy that limits the insurer's liability to those two areas if those areas could be clearly identified as being separate—for example, if there's a doorway setting them apart. I've seen it happen.

That's the starting point. You need to know the rules of the game and feel comfortable talking about these issues with your insurer.

TAKE YOUR TIME

At this point in the process, you need to build in time to do things right and in the right order. First, you need to do what we already talked about: adopt the right mind-set for your claim and then find somewhere safe, warm, and dry to live. It's incredibly difficult to deal with this stress in your life if you don't have those things sorted.

Another thing you'll want to do in a serious event like a fire or flood is to call upon many of the companies you rely on— your bank, your mortgage company, your energy company, even the local council—and let them know what's happened to see if you can get a suspension of your payments in order to manage your cash flow as effectively as possible. Some local councils will suspend council tax payments for a certain period of time, although that's down to the discretion of the local authority and is becoming rarer. When you're speaking to your bank, make sure you have access to emergency funding or an overdraft.

Once you are warm and dry, you can start to get familiar with your policy, looking out for all the potential difficulties that I've mentioned above. Again, take your time on this. There's no rush. The insurance company will want you to get them a list of items that are damaged or missing as soon as possible, but don't feel pressured by your insurer and rush into it. It's much more important to get it right, which is what we'll cover in the next chapter.

CHAPTER 3 RECAP

- **Get familiar with the key terms and conditions of your policy.**
- **Take your time and make sure you have the support you need to get through this situation.**

CHAPTER FOUR

Understand Your Losses

———

Have you ever tried to list everything you own? If your house has never been flooded or suffered from a fire, I'm guessing you haven't. Well, unless you have a photographic memory, it'll take some work to get a comprehensive list together.

The first thing I should mention here is that it's a lot easier to do this before you have a claim rather than afterwards. I've seen news stories warning of incoming hurricanes, telling people to go around their house with a video camera and record everything they own because, when the storm hits and they need to make an insurance claim, it makes things a hell of a lot easier.

In this chapter, I'll first talk about standard claims like fire and flood—for burglary, skip to the second part of this chapter, as dealing with burglaries is quite different to the usual process.

Before you send your claim to the insurance company, you have to be very clear about exactly what is damaged or has gone missing and the cost of replacing all those items. I've done this hundreds of times with my clients and developed some best practices on how to do this. If you're systematic and methodical about it and follow my advice, this part of the process will be much simpler.

STANDARD CLAIM SITUATIONS (FIRE, FLOOD, ESCAPE OF WATER)

1. ASSESS THE DAMAGE TO YOUR CONTENTS

Assuming now that the floodwaters have subsided or the fire is out and your home is safe to enter again, it's time to assess the damage, both to your contents and to the building itself. It's very rare, even in cases of fire or flood, that your entire home is destroyed, so your contents will usually still be in your home and visible to you.

Your insurer will send in a specialist cleaning and restoration company to do this, too, but it's important that you're there while the insurer is doing it. If the sofa has to be replaced, then they might just write "sofa" on their list, rather than specifying the type, colour, where you bought it, and so on. If you've bought a nice three piece suite from John Lewis, you don't want it to be replaced by the cheapest thing available in the next DFS sale.

In terms of contents, a lot of items will be classed as "beyond economic restoration," or BER. All that means is that, in the minds of the insurance company's cleaners, the item can't be restored and it's easier to just replace it with a new one. If you've suffered a serious fire or flood, this list will be long.

In some instances, it might be wise to let the cleaners try to restore something rather than replace it, depending on the basis of settlement. For example, clothing is usually subject to wear and tear, which means that, if you elected for a cash settlement, the cost of replacing the item would be more than the cash settlement you'd receive, so in that situation you'd do well to let them attempt to restore your clothing.

You should also be aware that restoration costs form part of the final settlement, so if your sum insured is low or inadequate, you'll only want to let your insurer attempt restoration if it's truly viable; otherwise, it could end up costing a lot of money.

The biggest issue you'll face with your BER list is that the list is written by technicians who have an interest in restoring your items and are not interested in the actual value of those items. While they do provide a service to you and the insurer in terms of listing the items that are BER, it will never be as comprehensive and detailed as a list you could create yourself, leaving you with the potential of having to prove your claim long after items have been disposed of.

So first, you need to know exactly what was in each room of your house and what is damaged. The easiest way to do this is to walk around with your phone. Download a voice recorder app if you don't have one already, and just go room to room and talk through what's there and what's damaged. You can get the audio transcribed later if you want, using a site like upwork.com or odesk.com to find someone to do that for you. Take pictures while you go round, too, especially if an item is particularly valuable.

At this point, when you're first making this list, there's no such thing as too small. If you go into your bathroom and see that your toothpaste is ruined and you need to buy another tube for £2, record that. It sounds stupid but if you go through all of your toiletries, once you add up everything there could easily be £200-300 worth of stuff there, especially if you have nice perfumes or aftershaves.

On the other end of the scale, for the expensive electronics like your widescreen TV or your PS4, the cleaning company will perform a Portable Appliance Test, or PAT. That sounds great, but actually all that the test says is whether the item is electrically safe, whether power is passing through it at that point in time. It doesn't assess functionality at all. In fact, I have a computer in my office that got through a PAT. You can plug it in and switch it on and a light will come on, but you won't see anything on the screen because there's something else wrong with it, thanks to water damage. So you need to make sure that your items pass what's called a "function test." And, if in doubt, you don't have to rely on the words of the restoration company.

Another area you should be wary of is the restoration costs of clothing and linen. Restoration is intended to (funnily enough) restore your items to the same or better condition than before your loss. The restoration company will usually send it to a specialist company or dry cleaners, for which they're charged a fee, and they'll add on their own profit margins, and charge it back to the insurance company. That's all well and good, but it's very easy for costs to quickly mount up, and all of a sudden you've got £5,000 worth of resto-ration costs for your clothes. Not to mention the fact that if you want your clothes replaced, that's unlikely to be on a new-for-old basis. So in this case it might be better to take the cash settlement of the cost of cleaning, rather than the restoration, because restoration is expensive and often won't actually get your clothes back to where they were before the incident (which, given the intent of restoration, means the insurers haven't actually met their obligations).

Once you've gone through your whole house, you should end up with a big list typed up on a spreadsheet of everything that is damaged and needs to be replaced or restored. You can do your own research on the replacement cost of each item. It's pretty easy these days with the internet and Amazon stocks almost everything, anyway—although be careful when getting prices off Amazon because they'll also show prices for second-hand items from resellers and you don't want to undermine the value of your claim in that way. Kelkoo.co.uk is also another useful aggregator site, especially for electricals and electronics.

The more detail you can provide on this list, the better. Don't write things like "TV"; instead, write "Samsung 32-inch LCD Smart TV" and write down the model number if you have it. If there's clothing, identify the labels where possible. Typically, once you're done with this list, it can be over 3,000 items long depending on the severity of the damage.

One thing you need to remember is that the replacement cost for a lot of items may well be lower than the price you paid for it. If you have a 60-inch TV that you paid £3,000 for, it might only cost £1,500 now—and the insurance company might be able to replace it for £1,200. You should record this as £1,500 on your spreadsheet, i.e. the cost you have sourced to replace the nearest equivalent. That way, you won't be disappointed with the insurer's offer later down the line because you won't be expecting £3,000. And if you went to Harrod's and paid £4,000 for it when the exact same item was available from John Lewis for £3,000, then sorry, you'll get the lower of the two. Your insurance company isn't there to pay a premium just so you can massage your ego and say you shop at Harrod's. They'll just replace your TV.

One other important thing to remember is about managing your cash flow during the life of your claim. Your insurer will often make payments to you before the final amount of the claim is decided to help you get back to normal quicker. But you need to make sure that you put this money aside and make sure you use it to carry out repairs and replace contents. Don't use it as cash flow to fund your day-to-day life or to go on holiday or anything like that. You need that money, so don't waste it.

I saw this happen when I was in New Orleans after Hurricane Katrina. We went to see a guy whose house had been completely destroyed. Nothing left at all. He showed up to meet us in a brand new red convertible, and on the back seat was a boxed-up 50-inch TV. And his words were, "I can't rebuild my house for the next six months. There's no builders available around here. So I thought I might as well have some fun in the meantime."

What he didn't understand was that your insurance policy is there to protect you and help you get your life back on track, not to give you some money to waste. Six months later that guy won't be happy when he has to sell his car and TV for half what he paid for them. Please don't make the same mistake.

2. ASSESS THE DAMAGE TO YOUR BUILDING

We've covered the contents. The claims for repairs to the building itself will be different. In a lot of situations, particularly after a flood, there are parts of a building that will quickly deteriorate if they're not repaired quickly. So in the instance of a flood, it might be your plastering or wallpaper that needs to quickly be dried, otherwise it will just get worse and worse and soon won't be able to be restored. In fact, in some instances the people doing the repairs may do what's called ROTAD work, Rip Out To Aid Drying, which means cutting out things like plaster to accelerate the drying process. Or they might just rip it out and put in new plastering or wallpaper, as it can be cheaper and quicker to just start over rather than dry and then repair certain work. For example, when I first started dealing with claims, I'd go to a house fire and insurers would have spent time and money burning off damaged paintwork on doors to then repair them. Now they just rip out the door and put a new one in.

One thing to note: make sure that before any restoration work starts, you take a reading of your gas and electricity meters. In the case of a flood, all of those dryers and restoration equipment that the contractors have will use a heck of a lot of energy, and you want to be reimbursed for that money, so you need to be able to show exactly how much energy they've used.

When you're dealing with extensive building damage, around £15,000 or more, the insurance company or the loss adjuster will recommend the use of a building surveyor and will usually introduce you to someone on their team. Now, fees for loss adjusting itself are quite small based on the responsibility they have to reinstate your home. So the way they make money is by using their own surveyor services, and they'll get paid 10 percent of the value of the building work as a cost that you are claiming and attributed to the claim against you as opposed to a cost incurred by insurers in administering your claim through your policy. But let's go back to the idea that this is your claim to make, not the insurance company's to dictate. In this instance, you should absolutely hire your own surveyor, with the insurance company's agreement, rather than use one of their team. That way, the surveyor will be answering to you and will have an explicit duty of care to you, and their fees will be paid accordingly under the policy as part of your claim.

Nowadays, insurers and their loss adjusters have panels of builders who have subscribed to undertake work on behalf of insurers based on nationally negotiated rates. The loss adjusters will specify what work is to be done and cost the work against those rates. The problem is that very few builders actually work that way.

For example, they will not be pricing to redecorate one wall of your house based on its size. Rather, they will work out how many days are needed and how much the materials used will cost. That makes a lot of sense, so you might be quoted, say, £400 by a decorator to repaint your front room, whereas the insurance company has negotiated a rate of around £4 per metre squared with their network builders irrespective of the size of the room, quality of the materials, and the real and practical costs of working in different parts of the country. This can mean the builder may be allowed, say, £120 to do the work. It doesn't take a genius to work out who is going to suffer because of this system!

To make matters worse, a lot of insurers will insist that £120 is sufficient to do the work and will therefore offer you a cash settlement of £120, leaving you with the dilemma of finding a builder to undertake the work or to wait until the next bank holiday to do it yourself! The other alternative is to let the builder used by the insurers do the work and then have the headache of fighting with them after the event to remedy all of the defects and inadequacies within the work.

BURGLARIES

Burglaries are a little different, so you need to take a different approach. The problem is that rather than listing everything you find that is damaged, you're trying to find what's missing—what's not there that should be.

Your policy is there to replace what's gone missing and put you in the same position financially, but what it won't do is fix the feeling of violation that you get from someone coming into your house, which is why feeling safe and secure again is where you need to start.

Now, when it comes to identifying what's gone missing, it will be difficult because, as the saying goes, "You can't prove a negative." Unfortunately, what you have is negative space, and so you need to identify what was there before. The only way you're going to do that is by doing an audit of your memories, trolling through them to try to identify what's gone missing.

One way to do that is to use your friends and family. Often they'll know you better than you know yourself, anyway. Don't be ashamed or embarrassed. They'll often say things like, "Say, where are those earrings that you bought me when I was 20?" and suddenly they'll realise that they've gone missing. Go through old photos, particularly from special occasions like birthdays and weddings where you're more likely to be dressed up smartly and wearing nice things. Look closely at the photos and think what you were wearing at the time. That will help you to identify some more items. Go back to Facebook and look in the background of some of your selfies. You'll probably see a lot of your possessions.

Just like with fire and flood claims, go back through your old bank and credit card statements. Look for big transactions or the names of jewellers on your statements. That will help you to identify some more items, too. It sounds daft but even go back onto your Amazon account and look at your purchase history. Check your emails for email receipts from other online retailers. All this will help you to build up a better picture in your mind.

As I said earlier, don't go to your friend and ask them to write you out receipts. It's not worth it, and insurers are wise to this and can often determine if the receipt isn't genuine. However, if your friend did genuinely supply you with items, then they can confirm the purchase by producing a duplicate receipt, if their systems allow, or write a letter confirming they supplied the item in question.

Also the truth is often stranger than fiction, so don't be embarrassed about the circumstances you bought an item (as long as it was legal). I have had clients who have bought really nice pieces of jewellery for far less than the item was worth to help out a friend who was in need of some cash. Others bought things at a discount because of friends who were able to supply goods cheaply through work schemes.

This sort of thing happens all the time and, as the policy is there to put you back in the same position you were had the incident not happened, insurers are then contractually obliged, subject to the policy limits, to pay the cost of replacing the items at whatever the cost is to them—be it greater or lower than the cost you paid.

You should also understand the regular *modus operandi* (MO) of the thieves in the area. Ask the police what items tend to be targeted. As I said, this is the thief's business and he doesn't want to get caught, so it's very unlikely that he will steal things that are difficult to sell on (or fence) or can be easily traced to you. In my experience, it is now much rarer for a TV to be stolen as they have become relatively cheap, so for a thief to sell it he is going to get very little money back but have a greater risk of being caught with such a large and bulky item.

I remember right at the depth of the recession in 2008-2009, when there were an awful lot of cash-for-gold adverts on TV, in newspapers, and on the radio, where they'd send you a prepaid envelope, you'd put your items in there and mail it to them, and you'd receive a cheque in the post a few days later. At the time, thieves would literally go into people's houses carrying a stack of these prepaid envelopes, stick the jewellery or watches straight into the envelope, and post them on their way home again. They could get rid of the items so quickly and have little chance of it being tied back to them. It was basically impossible to catch anyone with stolen goods in their possession.

This also sometimes happens with mobile phones, where there are websites that will pay you cash for recycling an old mobile. Lots of insurance companies now require you to notify your provider as soon as possible, even if it's one of those old mobiles that's just sat in a drawer somewhere. It still has a value, particularly if it's unlocked and not tied to a network anymore. If you're missing a mobile, phone your provider as soon as possible to notify them that it's gone missing so that they can block it on their end. A lot of insurers either won't pay your claim until that happens or they won't pay for any bills that have been racked up on your phone unless you tell them it's been stolen, so do that as soon as possible if a mobile is missing.

In terms of valuing your missing jewellery, unless you've had that particular item valued in the past or it's specifically identifiable, then you'll have to troll local jewellers or go and see if there's a jeweller who will give you current replacement prices for something comparable. The big high street chain Goldsmiths, and other similar chains, have great websites where you can enter the type of product you're looking for and they'll give you comparable prices.

The issue you'll have with jewellery is that the insurer can usually get a big discount, up to 30 percent or more, if they supply a replacement. So there will be some distress when it comes to settling a claim for jewellery because it will never marry up with your expectations—partly because of the insurer's discount and partly because of the sentimental value that is inevitably attached to certain items of jewellery, which an insurer can never replace. So manage your expectations when it comes to claiming for jewellery.

On other items, make sure you're getting the full value of what that item is worth. Don't just accept the insurer's valuation off the bat. If you think an item is worth more and you can back that up, then you should claim for that amount. Here's a good example: a client of mine just dealt with a burglary where one of his kids had three of his computer games stolen. When the insurer looks at that, they'll just say "computer game, they're worth about £20" and pay the same for each of them. It turned out that one of these games was rare—you can't buy it anywhere these days—and highly desirable, so it's actually worth about £125. If you leave it up to the insurer, you'll never get the full value you're after.

CHAPTER 4 RECAP

- **Now you need to understand your true losses.**
- **For contents, go from room to room with a voice recorder, talking through everything in order to jog your memory.**
- **Use old photos, bank statements, credit card bills, and any other documents as reminders of what you have bought and owned.**
- **Allow builders and restoration companies to move quickly to carry out any repairs needed.**

CHAPTER FIVE

Learn the Rules

—————

You need to understand the rules of the game that you're playing. Like I've already said, you're a novice at this, but the insurer plays this game every single day. You need to get familiar with the terminology, the clauses, every little detail of your policy, so that you know what you're talking about and can deal with the claim effectively. And the first place to start is by reading your policy itself.

Your policy is your contract with the insurance company. It lays out exactly what they will do, and exactly what you have to do, to stay within the limits of that contract and ensure it always applies. The problem is that it's not written for your benefit. It's written for the benefit of the insurance company. It's to protect them at the time when you need to call them into action. That might sound jaded but I've been in the industry for years and, sadly, that's the reality.

Policyholders don't always see it that way. You might think,

Hang on, Joel. I've been with the same company for 50 years. They used to come round and collect my premium every year and stop for a cup of tea. That may be true but the insurer is still going to write its terms and conditions to protect themselves and limit their liability wherever they can. That's just what they have to do when they're dealing with millions of pounds of premium and hundreds of thousands of customers. Like I said before, they are filtering for dishonest people because, in their view, there are plenty of those out there.

Luckily you can put in some time and research to fully understand your policy and, once you get to know some of the terminology, it actually becomes a lot easier. Here are some of the key things you need to understand.

CONTENTS VERSUS BUILDINGS

First things first: What type of policy do you actually have? Have you insured your building *and* contents or just one of the two? And what's the difference? Let me explain, because it's one of those things that seems obvious at first but is actually quite nuanced in places.

"Contents" is everything within your home. If you could pick up your house, turn it upside down, and shake it, then everything that fell out would be your contents. Everything that was left would count as "buildings." That includes fixtures and fittings. However, if something is secured to the walls of your home, even with a simple screw, it can be argued to be a building item. This is useful to know as, in my experience, people tend to have adequate building insurance cover but not usually sufficient contents sum insured.

There are a couple of additions to that: your carpets are considered contents, even if you won't take them with you when you leave. However, if the carpet has been stuck down and is fixed to the building, then it falls under your buildings policy, not your contents. Laminate flooring might be considered contents, unless it's been fitted underneath the skirting board. Then it becomes part of the building.

When it comes time to submit your claim to the insurer, there's going to be two distinct parts to your claim: the buildings and the contents. Take the time to read through your policy and understand what falls under each different part and, for that matter, what is not covered.

SUM INSURED

Your sum insured is essentially the total value up to which the insurer will pay out. Strangely, when people think about whether or not something is insured, they always think about a burglary and miss the idea of a total loss, where everything—and I mean everything—is gone. Instead you should ask yourself: If my house were completely destroyed and I was left with nothing except the clothes on my back and the key to my front door, would the amount I'm insured for be sufficient to replace everything as new? If the answer to that question is "no," then your policy isn't going to give you the level of cover that you expect, irrespective of whether 10 percent or 100 percent of your home is damaged. You are underinsured.

Different insurers have different ways of calculating and dealing with underinsurance. Some will apply the average principle. This means they will only pro-rate your claim in proportion to your sum insured and the actual value. So if your sum insured is £200,000 and it should have been £300,000, then the insurer will pay two-thirds of any claim. Depending on the degree of underinsurance, different policies will have different ways of phrasing it. Some will use the term "average," others will talk about "proportionality." Some may leave it open and just tell you that in the event of underinsurance, you won't receive the full value of your claim, but they won't at that point dictate the method of settlement. For example, the policy may revert to an indemnity policy, which means that the replacement value of items will be reduced by any wear and tear the insurer assumes to have taken place or the second-hand market value of items.

Most people these days will have a new-for-old policy—it's very rare to have an indemnity policy these days—so it doesn't matter if an item is 10 years old or 2 weeks old. The cost of replacing it is the cost of going out and buying it as new. So don't think *Oh, that's 10 years old. It's only worth a few quid now.* No, your insurer will go out and replace it as new. So when you're thinking about your sum insured, you need to ask: "How much would it cost to buy everything here, today, brand new?"

The easiest way to do that is to go room by room and do some guesstimates of what there was, making allowance for the things that are visible and what's in your cupboards. Don't miss those cupboards.

If you're underinsured but the insurer isn't settling based on averages, then they might do a couple of things. They may just settle your claim as you present it, depending on their thresholds for the claim value and the degree of underinsurance. They might offer you an indemnity settlement, which will reflect not the *replacement* value of the items but the *actual* value of the items as they stood at the time.

The worst case scenario is in extreme cases of underinsurance—and different companies will define that differently—where some insurers will avoid paying your claim entirely. Each insurer will have a particular degree of underinsurance at which they will decide to avoid the claim entirely rather than simply pro-rate your settlement.

In fact, insurers may try to void your claim if certain items exceed limits on your policy. I remember when gold prices shot up a few years ago, suddenly a lot of people found that their jewellery was underinsured. Insurers were trying to avoid paying claims based on underinsurance even in circumstances where the overall limit was sufficient, based on the single item limits or limits on valuables being insufficient.

Of course, even if you are underinsured, the insurer still has to abide by the principle of treating customers fairly, so if you do run into trouble, you can always take your claim to the Financial Ombudsman Service. They'll look at your circumstances and say, "Okay, this is a form of non-disclosure, but was it innocent non-disclosure? Was this customer trying to get a lower premium or were they just unaware of the full value of their building and contents?" If it's the latter, then FOS will likely find in your favour and the insurer will pay your claim anyway. Regardless, underinsurance can result in very painful situations when it comes to a larger claim, so be very careful that you're adequately insured.

As a small aside, that's one of the reasons I have the policy I do—I won't recommend a particular insurer, but look around and you'll find it. I have a policy with unlimited sums insured for buildings and contents and no single item limit, too. That happens to be the Marks and Spencer Premium policy but there are others, too. I have that level of cover because I've spent a lot of time and effort to build the life I want and I want to protect that. You're buying insurance for peace of mind so you might as well get a policy that gives you that, rather than buying the cheapest one off the shelf to satisfy your mortgage provider and ultimately protect you when the worst happens.

DEFINITIONS

That's your sums insured sorted. Next I'd look at the insurer's definitions, in conjunction with the method of settlement. For example, you want to look at your high-risk items. Firstly, how are they defined? It might just be jewellery and valuables like watches but other policies would include TV and audio equipment, computers, games consoles, and so on. One particular policy that I know of also extends that definition to include valuable personal possessions like sports equipment, musical equipment, and items that you might normally wear or carry, i.e. your clothing. So be very clear on what the definition is.

For high-risk items, you'll have an overall limit, and within that, you might have a single item limit as well. For example, your contents sum insured might be £100,000. Within that, you have a high-risk items limit of £30,000 and, within *that*, you have a single item limit of £5,000. Some insurers will also state that anything over a certain value will not be covered—irrespective of the limit—unless you meet certain conditions, such as having up-to-date valuations, having the item checked or appraised by a reputable jeweller, etc.

You'll want to look at what the different methods of settlement are for those high-risk items—whether cash or new-for-old and so on, and decide on what basis you want each item to be replaced. Like I mentioned earlier, if it's a priceless piece of family jewellery that can never be replaced, you might just want to take the cash, but if it's a Rolex watch that you like to wear, then replacement might be a better option. Also remember that some insurers will ask that you prove the value of the item and prove that you own it. It might rest on you to prove ownership rather than the insurer to disprove that you owned an item.

Another note on valuable items: some policies will want you to specify any item over a certain limit, say £1,500. And if you don't specify it on the policy, then it will be excluded from the claim. If you have an item that's worth £1,499, then they'll pay for it. If it's worth £1,501, then they won't—they'll either pay up to the limit or exclude the item. So you need to be very clear with the insurer the value that you want to claim for. At that point, you're claiming for what you think the item is worth.

If you have items that are valuable but don't fall into the category of "high-risk items," then always claim for them. Don't assume that just because they're expensive, the insurer won't pay for them. The old expression "If you assume anything, you'll make an ass out of you and me" applies to insurance claims, too. Always start by writing down your whole list, as I've outlined in earlier chapters, and then look at how your policy might apply to that list.

WARRANTIES AND CONDITIONS

Next, look for any expectations that the insurer might have for you. For example, you might find a good number of security conditions: types of locks, that your doors and windows have to comply with certain standards, and so on. What's important to remember here is that with regard to these conditions, an insurer can only refuse to pay your claim if you have materially breached one of these conditions and it is connected to the claim. That's a well-known principle among insurers and is actually part of the FCA's handbook.

Then you need to look at what information you'll need to provide to the insurance company in order to make a claim successfully. Under all policies, you have a full duty to provide as much help and assistance as reasonably required by insurance companies, whether those enquiries come from the insurer directly or from their loss adjuster. Of course, there's no strict definition of what is and isn't "reasonable." In the case of burglary, some insurance companies may ask you to fill in a Subject Access Request form, which allows them to get a copy of the police report to make sure it's consistent with the claim that you're making. That's reasonable. What is unreasonable is if the insurer asks you to turn out every drawer in your house. So don't put up with any nonsense— you have a duty to assist them but it's not a blank cheque for

BREACHES OF POLICY CONDITIONS

The Financial Conduct Authority (FCA) dictates the rules that insurance companies have to abide by. There's one in particular, under the Insurance Conduct of Business Rules (ICOBS), that is particularly relevant here. I don't expect you to learn all the rules off by heart, but this one is one you should know:

ICOBS 8.1.2: *Rejection of a policyholder's claim is unreasonable, except where there is evidence of fraud, if it is:*

...

(3) for breach of warranty or condition unless the circumstances of the claim are connected to the breach.

What that means in plain English is that if the insurer imposes certain conditions on you as part of your policy, and you don't do what they want, they can't reject your claim if your failure to carry out their instructions didn't impact whether or not you suffered a loss.

Here's an example. If you have a policy condition that says you should leave your security alarm on when you leave the house, and you fail to do so, and then your house gets flooded, the insurer can't refuse to pay your claim. The flood had nothing to do with you not putting your alarm on. That's an example of an immaterial breach. But if your policy says you need to have a certain type of lock on your doors and you don't, and then someone breaks into and exits your house through those doors, then that's a material breach.

them to abuse you and ask you everything and anything about your entire life. They have to treat you fairly and with an element of respect. They'll still be filtering for reasons not to pay you but, as I said earlier, there are only two grounds on which they can do that: fraud or breach of policy conditions.

Having said that, you should make it easy for the insurer to pay you. Give them everything they need and allow them to take their time to carry out their process. Let the claim take its natural course. If they have any questions related to the nature of the claim, like the circumstances, and they're looking to support that or support the content of your claim, then you've got no issues. If you feel a certain request is unreasonable and want to take a stance on it, hoping that the financial ombudsman will agree with you later down the line, you can do that, but it takes time and energy and gets you further away from your goal.

TRACE AND ACCESS

This is a very specific point that only applies to escape of water claims, but it's one you should be aware of. If you have a leak and there's water damaging your property, you have a responsibility to mitigate your loss immediately. Remember, you need to take all reasonable actions to do so, under your policy. So you need to carry out repairs to stop the leak.

Unfortunately, in a lot of cases, it's not immediately evident where the leak is coming from. Typically your water tank will be close to or above your bathroom, which will be above your kitchen—a lot of houses are built like that to minimise the amount of plumbing work that needs to be done. So if you've got water dripping into your kitchen or dining room, it could be coming from a few different places—the shower, the faucet, the toilet, a crack, a pipe, anything. Water will always take the path of least resistance, which isn't always the most obvious (or even visible) route.

Locating the source of that leak will inevitably be a systematic process of elimination. But any damage caused in getting access to the pipework in order to find that leak is not necessarily covered by the policy. The policy provides cover for the damage caused by the insured event, so damage caused in getting to the source to stop an event from causing damage is **not** covered.

Say you have to cut a hole in the ceiling to get to the source of a leak. The insurer will pay for the ceiling to be fixed if it was already damaged by water, but not if you have to do so to fix the leaky pipe. Also, they won't pay if you're just doing that to locate the leak or as part of a process of elimination...

...unless, that is, you have trace and access cover.

Trace and access cover provides insurance for fixing the damage caused in locating the leak, up to a particular limit. This is typically sold as an extension on a policy, although it's becoming more common on the higher-end insurance products. If you have a water leak, you must check whether or not you have trace and access cover. It then becomes crucial, when you're explaining to your insurer why you cut a hole in the ceiling, whether you did it to locate the leak—which is fine if you have trace and access cover—or whether you were doing it because that area had already sustained water damage, which will be paid for by all insurers. Think very carefully about what you should say here. If it's the latter, you need to demonstrate to the insurer that your ceiling has suffered from water damage. Think carefully about how that might be possible to do.

The other thing to watch out for with trace and access is that there is usually a financial limit to what the insurer will pay to repair water leak damage. If you have trace and access cover and your policy covers up to £5,000 of water damage, you might think *Great, I can spend £5,000 trying to find this leak.* Wrong. That £5,000 needs to cover not only the investigation but also the repairs that you caused by trying to find the leak. The damage caused by the water leak itself will still be dealt with as an escape of water claim.

MATCHING CLAUSE

Let's stick with the example of a water leak into your kitchen. Say you have a lovely matching kitchen with four or five different units in, and two of those have been damaged by the water leak. You would expect that your insurer would repair those two units or, if the units were beyond repair, that your insurer would replace your kitchen.

Wrong again. Most policies will have a matching clause that essentially states they will only pay for the items that have been damaged, not the items that match those that have been damaged, by uniformity of colour and design. If one chair out of your three piece suite has been damaged, they'll give you another chair, not a whole new three piece suite.

There are some policies—very few, mind you—where you can buy an extension to cover matching items like this. But they are few and far between.

Now, to get around this seemingly unfair practice, it has been put to a number of insurance companies as such: if your policy is to put you, as a claimant, back in the same position as you were previously, then you shouldn't have to suffer a financial loss. Therefore, if tomorrow you're sitting at home in your unmatched kitchen, you've not been put back in the same position as you were before because your unmatched kitchen means your home isn't worth as much as it was. If an estate agent came in, they'd use the lack of matching units as a reason to write down the value of your property.

What these people proposed to insurers was that the correct practice would be for the insurer to manufacture specific bespoke units at a premium to replicate what the units looked like prior to the damage. That would truly be putting you back in the same position as you were. But obviously the costs of doing so can be regarded as excessive, so typically what insurers will do as a compromise is pay 50 percent of the costs of replacing the rest of the undamaged units. That's a FOS guideline (although not a ruling), so some insurers will offer to do this without asking any questions, whereas others may require you to complain before they cede to this request.

Here's an example to illustrate this. If your kitchen costs £10,000 and 40 percent of that is damaged, then the insurer will pay you £4,000. That will fix your damaged units. Then they can give you a 50 percent contribution towards the remaining cost, which would be £6,000, for a total of £7,000.

You'll still need to put in a bit of your own money if you want everything to match—which is fair, because it will all be brand new. So you can either have unmatched units at no cost or a completely redone kitchen for £3,000 of your own money. Think back to one of the earlier principles: you need to understand what your goals are. This is a perfect example of that.

When you're doing your contents claim, you might have the same issue with your carpets. If you have the same carpet all throughout the house but only part of it is damaged, then the matching clause may apply. But what the insurers will do in the case of carpets is look for a natural threshold, like a door or a door bar, that can break up the area and limit their liability. If you have the same carpet in your living room and your hall but there's a door in between the two, then they might just replace the carpet in your living room, for example.

CHAPTER 5 RECAP

- **You need to become familiar with the particulars of your insurance policy.**
- **Understand what you will be claiming for under contents or buildings.**
- **Look closely at your sums insured and limits on valuables and single items.**
- **Check what warranties and conditions have been imposed and assess if they are relevant to your claim.**
- **If you have a water leak, check if you have trace and access cover.**
- **When claiming for part of a matching set, check if your policy includes a matching clause.**

CHAPTER SIX

Present Your Claim

This is where all your effort comes to fruition. You've read your policy cover-to-cover, every word of it. You understand the difference among replacement, indemnity, reinstatement, and cash settlement. You're now an expert on the whole process.

It's time to gather all your information and present your claim to the insurance company.

This starts with the list of items that we talked about in an earlier chapter. This should be a meticulous, detailed spreadsheet with everything that anyone could ever want to know about that item in order to identify it. You can't just say "I had a steel bracelet watch" and then ask for £1,000 for it. What you need to do is give the insurer all the info they'd need to give to their own valuers to identify and accurately value whatever it was that was stolen or damaged, as well as showing the provenance of any item, i.e. where did it come from?

To do this, you'll need to use your aide–mémoires. Use your audio recordings that you made when you were walking around your house. Use your Facebook pictures, the digital record of your life. Use your credit card receipts and bank statements. Ultimately, for that same watch, you need to know: Did it have a round face or a square face? What type of movement did it have? What make was it? What type of case was it? Was it gold-plated or solid gold or stainless steel? Did it have numbers or roman numerals on the face? Did it have a date indicator? Really get into the nitty gritty. It should be so detailed that someone reading your description could pick the item out of a catalogue.

This doesn't just apply to high value items; this is for everything. You have to do this because of how insurance companies validate your items, which is usually through an outsourced company. If you don't give this level of detail, then often those outsourcers will send you a little guide on how to identify your item and then they'll talk you through that guide over the phone. So if you were talking about jewellery, then they might send you a guide to help you identify different types of generic jewellery: chains, chain widths, stone sizes, stone cuts, and so on. What this means is that the more information you can give them upfront, the less time you'll need to spend on the phone going through these sorts of telephone interviews, which can quickly get tedious and time-consuming. And it also means that it's easier for them to identify exactly which items you own so there's less discussion of exactly what level of final settlement you should get.

What these outsourced third parties will also do is validate the information that you're giving to the insurer. So for example, there was a time when people would steal a lot of CDs, DVDs, and computer games. When listing what was stolen, people often just listed the most recent games that they could find on Amazon or couldn't remember all 60 DVDs that they owned and so made some up. Then when their claim was being validated, there'd be some red flags because people were claiming that a particular game or DVD had been stolen—and it hadn't even been released at the time of the theft.

But like I've said before, the insurer will understand that people don't always have perfect memories. If we did (and if everyone were honest), then the insurer could just take your word for everything. Unfortunately that's not the case, so spend some time online doing your research, making your own notes, and making sure that you've got as much info as possible. You also want to make sure you're being consistent. If you say one thing, then contradict yourself later on, that's something that will get picked up, and it's an indicator of fraud. If we go back to the example of a watch for a moment, if you really had a watch that you're claiming £1,000 for and all of a sudden you said, "Oh, actually it was a blue face and not a champagne-coloured face," you're going to raise suspicions. That doesn't mean that you're not entitled to make a mistake because, as I just said, you don't have a perfect memory. But when you are supporting your claim by the photographs and other documents that you may have in your possession, it will help you narrow down and confirm exactly what was what.

So spend a bit of time online—and the internet is an incredible resource these days—getting as much info as possible, getting the right prices, and so on.

USEFUL RESOURCES FOR VALUING ITEMS

- amazon.co.uk
- ebay.co.uk
- watchfinder.co.uk
- hsamuel.co.uk
- ernestjones.co.uk
- johnlewis.com
- kelkoo.co.uk
- goldsmiths.co.uk
- tiffany.co.uk
- cartier.com
- currys.co.uk
- argos.co.uk
- selfridges.co.uk
- austinkaye.co.uk
- fellows.co.uk

One thing to note when it comes to jewellery in particular: don't limit your online research to places that are just selling the items as new. Go to some of the second-hand suppliers and other buyers, where they can often identify historic pieces, watches, pens, or other slightly more obscure items like that. Ebay is also a useful resource for finding item valuations. You can look at past auctions to find out the final purchase price of an item.

PROVING OWNERSHIP

Assuming you now have a long and detailed list of items,

with credible and full descriptions, you'll now need to prove as best you can that you owned those items at the time. So you need to record and document—again, making it as easy as possible for the insurer to pay you—any receipts, photographs, instruction manuals, and so on. Anything that will be an indicator that you owned the item.

Insurers will also want to know the provenance of an item. Where did you get it from? Did you buy it or was it a gift? If you bought it, where from? If it was a gift, who bought it for you? Note that there's no point saying it was a gift from someone in the same household, as you're all claiming under the same policy. If your spouse bought you some jewellery—a nice ring or a new watch—where did they get it from?

Don't be afraid of the truth here, as I mentioned earlier, as long as it's legal. It's unbelievable the number of people who have bought high value items from a friend who is a little short of cash and then don't want to admit that when they need to claim for those items. Your policy is there to replace your items. It's not a matter of whether or not you bought it at the going rate or below that because an opportunity came up. Don't come up with some BS story that won't stand up to scrutiny. It's okay to say, "You know what? My friend was short of cash so I paid him £50 for his watch. Yeah, it was a great deal, but now it's gone missing and I need to claim for it." You're entitled to the full replacement value, whatever that may be, and not just the £50 you paid for it.

So now your list is complete. If this is a burglary we're talking about, you need to give a copy of your list to the police, too. It'll be recorded by them and then verified by your insurance company that the police's information matches theirs. Insurers generally have an agreement with the National Police Chiefs' Council that the police will furnish the insurers with this information, but some insurers will also ask you to complete an Appendix D form (a Subject Access Request form, which is designed to comply with data protection legislation) for you to give your permission to have this data shared.

On this list, be sure that you're claiming for damages, too. It's not unusual for thieves to cause damage, particularly at the point of entry. If they've smashed a window to get in and there's glass all in the carpet, then the insurer should pay to either have the glass removed or, if that's not possible, to replace the carpet. If they've smashed down a door, you can get the doors and locks replaced. Likewise if some furniture is damaged, then that should be paid for. You're entitled to be put back in the same place as you were before the event.

What they won't do is pay for you to upgrade your home security. That's an improvement, not a replacement. It's totally understandable to want added security after you've been burgled—most people do—but you'll have to pay for that out of your own pocket.

OTHER PARTICULARS

When it comes to repairing water damage, the cleaners will be trying to dry out your property as much as possible with dehumidifiers. The problem is that those dehumidifiers will dry anything and everything. Most of your possessions have some level of moisture in them, anyway, so you want to be careful that your house or your possessions that weren't damaged by the water don't get damaged by the dehumidifying process—but if that does happen, you can claim for that damage, too. What you want to do is wait until the property is completely dry; you'll get a dryness certificate from the cleaning company at that point. That's when you can assess the damage and make the claim.

In fact, that's a general principle: if someone instructed by or on behalf of the insurer causes any damage in carrying out any repairs or restoration, then you're absolutely entitled to recover that money as part of your claim. If it's your own builder or cleaner that you're instructing and he causes some damage, you'll have to pay for that yourself, or make a separate claim under the accidental damage part of your policy, if you have that extension. There's also a distinction here between something failing to respond to restoration due to the extent and nature of the damage, as opposed to a failure of the restoration process itself (e.g. shoddy work). If it is the latter, and you're using your own contractors, you might be left pursuing your contractors for that damage. See the sidebar *"Should you use the insurer's contractors or find your own?"* for more information on choosing whether or not to appoint your own people.

As a general rule, never be afraid to ask if you can claim for something. Do not do the loss adjuster's job for them and limit your claim yourself. Now, that doesn't mean that you should claim for things that aren't damaged. But it's better to ask and be told "no" than to not ask at all. The loss adjuster's job is to literally adjust your loss on behalf of the insurance company. This is your claim to make, not theirs to dictate, so it's up to you to assess your losses and present them to the insurer or the loss adjuster first.

Typically insurers will ask you to get two estimates for all of your reinstatement work to your buildings. They'll want you to make sure that both quotes are consistent, too—essentially, that you're comparing apples with apples. Ask your contractors for a breakdown of the work that they're doing and the cost for each aspect. They might also get their own builders in to do some costing, too.

You'll want to look very closely at their costs. Insurers will typically have set rates for certain types of work and often it's difficult to find contractors who can do the work for the rates specified by the insurer.

You'll also need to get quotes for other expensive items like carpets. The insurer's specialist suppliers will come down and provide a quote direct to the insurance company. They will then provide a voucher so you can replace the carpet through suppliers who subscribe to the particular scheme. This is why you should always keep a sample of your carpet if it's being replaced or written off and ensure that you get a comparable carpet. Should you choose to get a better carpet or change it for, say, wooden flooring, you can use the voucher and benefit from the discounts that the insurer can get from suppliers like that, too.

SHOULD YOU USE THE INSURER'S CONTRACTORS OR FIND YOUR OWN?

It depends. I know, that's not a very helpful answer, but it really does depend on a lot of different factors.

Your default position should always be to take ownership of the claim. So in general, I'd recommend engaging with your own contractors wherever possible.

The problem is down to the set rates that insurers have for certain types of work. Often these can be very low. The reason for this is that insurers will have national networks of contractors that they use on a regular basis. Local firms want to be part of these networks because, naturally, insurers send them a lot of work. But in exchange for being part of the network, the contractor has to accept the rates set by the insurer, who is out to cut costs and save money wherever they can.

That problem is compounded by the fact that the initial estimate of what work is required is done by the loss adjuster, who isn't a skilled tradesman and often underestimates the extent of the work.

Here's an example. I'm working with a client whose living room wall was damaged. It needs repairing and new wallpaper put in. The loss adjuster came onto the site and put all the work needed into his system and the specified rate came out at £28 per square metre. We cannot get a contractor to do the work for anywhere near that. The closest we came was for someone who would do it for about £40 per square metre—almost 50 percent more expensive. That's a huge difference.

In general, you want to maintain ownership of the claim and use your own contractors. But in situations like this where it's impossible to find anyone to do the work at those rates, then you should let the insurer use their own contractors and let them deal with that headache.

There's another factor to take into consideration too, though, because it's not always just about the money. Sometimes it's about having the work done to the correct standards and in the most effective manner. If that means paying some money out of your own pocket because the insurer's set rates are too low, then you need to decide if that's a price worth paying, and if it is, use your own contractors.

If the rates set by the insurer are very low, then their contractor—who is obligated to carry out the work at those rates by virtue of the fact that they are in the insurer's network—might try to find ways to cut corners, get the job done quicker, and not take as much care and attention as they should. Thankfully, there's a fallback. The insurer is obligated to put you back in the position you were in before you suffered the loss, so if their contractors haven't done that, then you just need to pick up the phone, call your insurer, and tell them that, and they're obligated to come back and fix it.

In the event that you do actually engage with your own contractor to carry out the building work within the valuations set by the insurer, you want to make sure you're contracting with someone who you know and trust, and have possibly worked with before, rather than someone that you've just found on Google or in the Yellow Pages. You still want to make sure that the job is going to be done right. If you can't find someone who you know and trust, then you'd be better off going with the insurer's contractors.

If you do use your own contractor or you've taken a cash settlement, it mostly lets the insurer off the hook if any additional work is necessary later down the line or if the work is defective in any way. But there's still a way around that if you need it. The Financial Ombudsman Service has said that in situations where the insurer or loss adjuster is "controlling" the work of the contractor, it doesn't actually matter whether or not they have a contractual relationship. The insurer still has the same level of responsibility when it comes to seeing that the job is completed properly. By "controlling," they mean that the insurer (or their representatives) is dictating the level and scope of work or the value of the claim being presented.

If you'd rather take the cash and negotiate your own deal, then you should ask your insurer for a cash settlement because a lot of independent carpet suppliers pay too much to insurers to be one of their preferred suppliers. Here's how to decide whether or not you want to take a cash settlement or let the insurer's suppliers carry out the work for you:

1. Do I think I can get a better value deal with the insurer's suppliers than with the cash in my pocket?

2. Do I want to replace the item in question?

If the answer to either of those is "no," then you should ask for a cash settlement.

If you choose to do that, just make sure that you're getting exactly what you want—that it's the right carpet and the right quality and so on. But I wouldn't recommend doing this for exactly the same reasons as I suggested when it comes to organising the builders. Why do you want the extra hassle and work? Let the insurance company deal with it.

Remember, insurers don't have to abide by the method of settlement that you want, but most will usually accommodate you if they can and if it reduces their liability.

REPLACEMENT ITEMS VERSUS CASH SETTLEMENTS

When you're presenting your claim, don't just mark each item on the list with whether you'd like the cash or a replacement. It doesn't work like that. Instead, what the insurer will do is make a proposal to you in terms of cash settlements for each item that cannot be replaced. For example, in my office I have a really nice massage chair—which cost me way too much and doesn't do what it should—but I know that my insurer does not have a specialist supplier for this particular chair. They might be able to get a 25 percent discount on furniture in general but that's irrelevant in this case because they can't replace this particular item. So they'd have to pay me the full replacement value, what it would cost me to go out today and buy another one, brand new. This is also the case with jewellery from certain high-end suppliers like Tiffany as well as antique or unique items. The insurer can't replace the specific items in question. So always make sure the insurer gives you all your options.

You'll want to think about this carefully. Although it sounds great to have all your items replaced, there is a certain amount of coordination that you have to do. Imagine getting all these different items delivered to your house at all hours of the day. You might be expecting a delivery at 9 a.m. and it doesn't come until late afternoon (we've all been there) and you've had to miss work for it. Then when it finally comes, you realise that it's the wrong colour or the wrong size and you have to send it back and go through the whole process again. Now multiply that across several different items. So think carefully about which items you really want replaced and which you'd be happy to think about a cash settlement for. Also, do you really want all your items replaced? I know I've bought plenty of stuff in the past that I don't really want and wouldn't really miss if it were gone. Those items are perfect candidates to be taken as a cash settlement rather than a replacement.

ACCOMMODATION COSTS

Like I said back at the start of the claims process, your insurer will pay for you to find alternative accommodation similar to the standard of your own home. What you need to watch out for is that there is usually a limit to the amount they'll pay.

Take a client of mine. Their house needed to be knocked out and repaired. There was some serious and extensive work needed, and the insurer reckoned it would take 6 to 8 months, but we decided to be cautious and plan around 10 months of alternative accommodation.

Their policy would pay for up to £25,000 and 12 months of alternative accommodation. Great! They could move out immediately and spend over £2,000 a month on accommodation and be absolutely fine.

Unfortunately, the building work actually took 15 months. But what we did was not have them move out immediately when the building work started. There was work that could be done while they were still in the house, so we made sure that the insurer did that work first, and that my clients only moved out when they had to. That way, the clock on the 12 month limit didn't start ticking until a few months after the building work had started.

So don't assume that the insurer will give you a blank cheque for accommodation. They will pay for all the additional costs associated with moving but it will all come under the accommodation costs limit. Things like your gas, electric, and council tax: if they increase as a result of having to move, the insurer will cover the increase. But that all falls under the same financial limit, so just be aware of that.

Not every cost associated with moving out will be admissible. For example, insurers will contribute to your food expenses if you have had to move into a hotel for the short term. However, the amount received is unlikely to be anywhere near the costs you incurred. The insurer will assume that you would have had to have eaten, anyway!

One thing you can discuss with your insurer is storage for your contents. If all your items have to go into storage for a number of months—which costs money—then ask them whether the items went into storage to allow you to move or to enable the building work to take place. If it's the latter, then those storage costs form part of the claim for building costs, not accommodation costs. You can shift those costs to a different part of the policy with a higher limit.

CHAPTER 6 RECAP

- List all your contents together in a large spreadsheet with as much detail as you can.
- Pull together any documentation or proof you might have as evidence of an item's value and to prove ownership.
- Consider what items you'd like replaced versus what items you'd like to take a cash settlement for.

CHAPTER SEVEN

The Loss Adjuster

Loss adjusters are like soldiers. They want to do the right thing—in this case, pay you what you're owed—but really they are just following orders. They have a process and a chain of command that must be followed, above all else. Their process is structured in such a way that they are filtering for reasons not to pay you, so you need to have everything in order first.

I know that is annoying. Just following orders doesn't really cut it when we're talking about people's lives that have been affected by a loss. You want to be heard and you want your insurer to respect your needs, rather than applying a process and trying to fit you into a box. But, unfortunately, that's the state of the industry at the moment, so you should be prepared for it.

At no point when I'm dealing with a loss adjuster do I ever want to be less than 100 percent prepared. Even when I'm dealing with my best friend, who's a loss adjuster, I am nothing but comprehensive because one day he might be unwell or get a new job or get the sack and suddenly the claim gets passed to someone else, and I don't want to take any chances.

The loss adjuster's role used to be to take your claim and adjust it to fit the policy—effectively representing the insurance company in all of their needs. But that's changed a lot over time. Now loss adjusters will usually have delegated authority from the insurer to handle claims in their entirety, up to a certain limit. For all intents and purposes, they are the insurance company. And they'll have a service agreement with the insurer which dictates how they need to perform. That impacts how they behave towards you so in turn you need to be confident when dealing with them—and the way to do that is to be completely prepared.

What you should also understand is that the loss adjuster's approach of just following orders means that if you're angry or frustrated, do not argue with or take it out on the loss adjuster. It's the process that's the problem, not the person. Stay calm and be civil and professional at all times.

FIRST ENCOUNTER

When they first come into your home, they'll be looking around as a fact-gathering exercise as well as giving practical direction on the claim and how it's going to happen. They'll do fact-gathering as a way of validating that you haven't failed to disclose certain things on the policy and that you've complied with the relevant terms and conditions. They have to check that the damage you're claiming for is as a result of an insured event—and they'll be looking for a way of explaining the damage through something that isn't insured.

They'll look at you as an individual, too. Are you the type of person who an insurer would want to deal with? Are there any reasons around that might cause to inflate a claim or have a claim occur where you might benefit? Are you having money troubles? Have you ever been in trouble with the police? They might not ask these questions outright but they'll be looking around your house for anything that might indicate as such to determine what level of moral hazard you pose. And what they will ask you is their standard checklist of questions that screen for potential fraud—although remember that there are only a few ways for them to check the accuracy of your answers, hence why you'll be asked about County Court Judgements (CCJs) and bankruptcies, as this is information that's publicly accessible.

MANAGING THE CLAIM

Once all that is done and the loss adjuster is satisfied that your claim is genuine, their role shifts to managing the whole process up to the settlement of your claim. It used to be the case that the loss adjuster had a duty of care to you as well as to the insurer, but that's not really the case anymore. Some genuinely will have your interests at heart and advise you if you're not claiming for everything you should be. But those are the exception rather than the rule, mainly because loss adjusters aren't as skilled, experienced, or well-paid as they used to be. Nowadays most loss adjusting firms are paid a small, flat fee per claim from the insurer, so they have an incentive to do the bare minimum possible while still meeting their service level agreement with the insurer.

As a policyholder, you don't have a contractual relationship with the loss adjuster. What you do have is an implied obligation under your policy to provide them with as much help and assistance as possible. But they don't have a duty to you at all. In fact, they are more likely to see you as their next meal ticket. Because they only get paid a flat fee per claim, some loss adjusters will have their own building surveyors and cleaning, repair, and restoration companies that they use to carry out any work on your home, which means they can then send that bill to the insurer and make more money that way. This is very common these days. Or they'll have a network of builders that they use and get referral fees of around 15 percent each time they send some work to one of those builders.

Now that all sounds very jaded and it is a little unfair because the loss adjustors only get paid at the time your claim is settled and they are regularly audited, too. So it is in their interests to have your claim settled quickly and correctly— but only by virtue of their agreement with the insurer, not because it's the right thing to do or because they're looking out for you. They're acting within the letter of the agreement, not the spirit of the agreement.

As an example of this, a lot of my clients often get letters from a loss adjuster which essentially say: "We have been instructed by your insurer to act on their behalf. We tried to contact you by telephone but haven't been able to reach you. Please call us to make an appointment for one of our adjusters to come out and see you." I'll tell you that in 80 percent of these cases, my clients didn't receive a phone call. But by writing that on the letter, the loss adjuster can say that they met their service level agreement with the insurer that says they have to make first contact within five days or so. They're just trying to hit their targets, ignoring the actual purpose of the process, which is to get started with the claim as soon as possible.

HOW TO TREAT THE LOSS ADJUSTER

Having said all that, even if the loss adjuster is just a soldier following orders, when he's in your house, you should treat him like a guest in your home. You've done all this preparation and time-consuming work, and the point of that is to make the loss adjuster's job as easy as possible and not give him any reason to dither or doubt you. Remember, you're not interested in the process; rather, you're interested in the outcome. What you need to do is smooth out that process and give the loss adjuster—who in this instance is the gate-keeper—all the help and assistance he needs to deal with your claim.

That doesn't mean you should be overly deferential and give him the keys to the castle. If he asks for a cup of tea, give him the cheap biscuits and not the hobnobs. If he asks you a question, just answer it honestly and directly. Don't embellish or go off on a tangent because you'll just waste time and open up other lines of questioning. If it's an irrelevant question, don't answer it. All the conversation between you and the loss adjuster should focus on:

- Who you are

- The circumstances of your claim
- The subject matter of your loss

Anything outside of those three headings is superfluous and might open the door to further enquiries. You should be polite and civil and give him exactly what he asks for—and no more.

Likewise, they should treat you with respect, too. The FCA has an over-riding principle that firms must "treat customers fairly" and the definition of that is pretty broad. If the loss adjuster is being rude or seems to be having a bad day and is taking it out on you, then just call the meeting to an end. You're perfectly within your rights to do that. Just make sure that if you do, you phone your insurer and tell them what happened and why you ended the meeting. Otherwise it might go down as a red flag against you, as it looks a bit suspicious.

The problem you're facing here is that loss adjusters often have an incentive to refer you to a fraud unit. They will never admit that they have quotas for this, but I have a suspicion that they do. Insurers have agreed that where a claim is particularly complex and fraud is suspected, they'll pay for a special investigator, an SI. Just like how loss adjusters can make money from either appointing their own builders or getting a referral fee from a builder, they can do the same with special investigators. So they have an incentive to play up the fraud potential of each claim in order to make money off it. This is why you need to do everything you can to play down the fraud potential of your claim.

Also, make sure you're asking him questions, too. What are the next steps? What's the process? How long will that take? When will I hear from you next? Make sure that you're informed and up to speed. I'll say it again: this is your claim to make, not the insurer's to dictate.

NEXT STEPS

Once the loss adjuster has been round to your house and determined that everything's in order, he'll start to progress the claim. For example, if it's a burglary, he'll report back to his central team of adjusters and admin staff, potentially contact the police to verify the list of stolen items, appoint a jewellery consultant and an electrical supplier, and so on. He might ask you for additional documentation or bank records to prove ownership of an item. Again, be civil, and give him what he asks for as quickly as possible.

When he's completed all his enquiries, he'll come back to you and make a proposal to either replace all your items, give you a cash settlement, or some combination of the two. If you want cash, don't be afraid to ask for it, but remember that the level of cash settlement might be less than it would cost you to go and replace an item in the shop because of the level of discounts the insurers can get from their suppliers.

If the claim seems to be taking a long time, much longer than you'd expect, then it might be one of two reasons. Firstly, sometimes claims can take a while to process—especially if the loss adjuster has to refer matters to the insurer, for example. There's some back and forth, which adds time in. Always ask why there is a delay and if you can do anything to expedite the process. If you feel the delay is unreasonable, go ahead and register a formal complaint with your insurer.

The second reason for delay is that the insurer suspects you of fraud. Insurers know that claims have a natural attrition rate, that over a long enough period people will have had enough and just want to settle to get it over and done with— or, if the claim is fraudulent, the fraudster will just drop the claim. So they'll often delay in cases where they suspect fraud. But they can't refuse to pay your claim unless they can prove fraud, which they won't be able to do if you're making an honest claim. The insurer might say to you "We believe this is fraud, so withdraw your claim" and some people will in fact drop their claim.

If this seems to be happening to you, don't get frustrated. As I've already said, the insurer can only refuse to pay if there has been a breach of policy conditions or if they can provide fraud. You can turn around and say exactly that to them. Phone them up and say, "You've accepted the claim that you're paying, so you agree there is no breach of policy conditions. All that leaves is fraud, and if it's fraud, please prove it to me." Once you do that and submit a formal complaint, in writing, that puts them on an eight-week countdown to either prove fraud or pay your claim, and if they don't do it, you can go to the ombudsman.

Having said that, that should be a last resort. If you do everything right, being neither too open nor too combative, giving them all the help they need and no more, you should get through it just fine and get the result you want.

It's almost time to put this whole incident behind you.

CHAPTER 7 RECAP

- The loss adjuster is like a solider. He's just following orders.
- That means you shouldn't take any chances. Make sure you have everything you need and that your claim is watertight.
- Be civil, polite, and courteous and give them all the information they ask for—and no more.
- Don't get frustrated if your claim seems to be taking a long time.

CHAPTER EIGHT

Wrapping Things Up

If you're surprised by the insurer's offer, you've done something wrong.

All this preparation you've done—all the notes, research, documentation—should present the insurer with enough information for you to receive a settlement that you expect. You should know exactly how they'll apply the rules and particulars of your policy and the different settlement options and the discounts that insurers might apply in the event of a cash settlement.

When you get your settlement offer, you need to think in particular about those discounts that insurers get (which can be in excess of 30-40 percent on items like jewellery). A mistake I see people make all the time is getting hung up on the price rather than the specification of an item. If your TV cost you £1,000 a few years ago and now the insurer is offering you £400, don't get annoyed—look at the spec of your old TV and what you can buy brand new today for £400. You'll be surprised.

This is most common on jewellery. When you're buying a nice ring or necklace from a retailer, remember that he's the last man in the supply chain. The manufacturer and the wholesaler both have their own margins as well, so your insurer can save a lot of money by going direct to one of those two. If you've spent a month's salary on an engagement ring and you're only getting offered two weeks salary for it, you'll be annoyed, but that is genuinely what the insurer would pay for that item. These jewellery manufacturers buy gold chains by the mile, so not all of the items in a jewellery store are unique. The special engagement ring you bought might actually be quite easy to replace. However, if you can demonstrate that your piece was so unique and individual that it can't be replaced just like that, then the insurer might not be able to get the same level of discount, so they'll have to give you an amount closer to the actual retail cost. Unfortunately, it's not always easy to do that after the fact. But the more information, documentation, pictures, details, or receipts that you have, the easier it will be to identify the exact item that you had—otherwise you will ultimately have to settle for a compromise between your (fallible) memory and what the insurer's jewellery consultant comes up with.

In cases where you do get offered a replacement item—and this applies to all items, not just jewellery—it's up to you to be the arbiter of whether or not that replacement item is good enough. The insurer simply hasn't abided by its duty and contractual obligation to replace the item. Nonetheless, you should let the insurer try and replace the item since it's on them to replace it even if the replacement ends up costing more than you're actually insured for because they have elected to reinstate you by way of replacement, which means they have to live up to that obligation. A client of mine had insured a diamond ring for £10,000 which she had bought in Amsterdam and paid for in euros—but two years later, when it was stolen, the changes in exchange rate and the market price for diamonds meant that to replace it would actually cost £15,000. I told her that if she settled in cash, she'd only get £10,000, which wouldn't be enough to replace the item, so she elected to let the insurer try to replace it, which they did in the end.

Another reason why replacement is good: if you want to improve an item, you can still benefit from the insurer's discount. Say your TV was a 32-inch that would cost £500 at John Lewis. Your insurer might be able to replace it for £400. But instead, you want a 40-inch TV that would cost £700. Your insurer can probably get it for £550. So all you need to pay is the difference between your insurer's cost of replacement (£400) and your insurer's cost of the improved item (£550). It will only cost you £150 to upgrade, whereas the difference in retail price is actually £200, so you're benefitting from the insurer's discount.

DEALING WITH LOW OFFERS

If your insurer does surprise you and offer you a cash settlement for less than you'd expected, you should go back and test them. Ask them to explain exactly how they arrived at that valuation. They should walk you through exactly what they've done to calculate that offer and you can challenge them on each individual part of that.

But if you're still not happy with their offer after that, you have three options:

1. Accept it and quietly walk away with their proposed settlement.

2. Sue the insurer to enforce your rights under your contract, as is your right under contract law.

3. Make a formal complaint to the insurer and refer that complaint to the Financial Ombudsman Service.

The first is easy—you don't need my advice on how to do that. The second is beyond the scope of this book—you'll need a contract lawyer. The third option is where I can offer some assistance.

Every complainant has the right to refer a case to the Financial Ombudsman Service, the FOS. The FOS was set up by parliament to be the arbiter of disputes between consumers and financial services companies. It's free (for the consumer) and its rulings are binding on companies.

But for your complaint to go to FOS, you first have to formally make a complaint to your insurance company. Instructions on how to do that will be in your policy wording—in fact, they have to be in your policy wording by law. It's usually a call to the customer services department or an official letter to the CEO, something like that.

When making your complaint, you have to do three things. You have to:

1. Make a broad complaint about how you're being treated

2. Be specific on the issues about which you're complaining

3. Be clear about the outcome that you would like

FOS always makes their ruling based on the distinct issue of the complaint and whether or not a customer is being treated fairly, and so you want to say exactly what it is that you feel the insurer is doing wrong that you would like to be addressed and why this is unfair.

That sounds odd, so here's an example. Say you're dealing with a fire and the restoration of your sofa hasn't been good enough. Your complaint to your insurance company should say these three things:

1. I feel that you are treating me unfairly. Under the policy, you are obligated to put me back in the position I was in before the incident happened, and you haven't done that. (Broad complaint)

2. Specifically, the restoration of my furniture has been unsuccessful and is well below the standard I would expect. Because of this, I am worse off than before. (Specific issue)

3. I would like either a replacement sofa or a cash settlement instead in order to fully indemnify me. (Outcome)

Focus on these three things and these three things only. When people are writing a complaint letter to their insurer, they often feel the need to document every single little thing that has gone wrong—a phone call that came at 2 p.m. rather than 1 p.m. as promised, a letter that was received a day late— rather than the crux of the matter. Everything outside of those three key points is just irrelevant noise. Don't bother with it.

Submitting a formal complaint like that starts the clock on the insurer. They have eight weeks to come back to you with a satisfactory result and resolve the complaint. Usually they'll try to do just that, especially if you have been clear about why you're complaining and the outcome that you'd like. Each complaint that gets referred to FOS actually costs the insurer about £500, so they have an incentive to resolve your complaint before that happens. But if they don't manage to do that, don't worry. Now you can refer your complaint to FOS.

You can submit your complaint to FOS online—just go to financial-ombudsman.org.uk—or telephone them. Again, details of how to complain to FOS have to be in your policy wording by law.

The first stage in the process is for an adjudicator to look at your complaint. Often they'll find in your favour at this stage, but if not, you can appeal this adjudication to have your complaint referred to a full ombudsman.

Referring your complaint to FOS has a few advantages over suing the insurer in court. Firstly, FOS is making a decision over, broadly, whether or not the customer has been treated fairly. A court would be making a specific decision over a point of contract law or tort law. Secondly, decisions at FOS are made by ordinary men and women based on a reasonable assessment of the circumstances, rather than by judges who are bound by years of legal precedent and statute law. Simply, it's easier to win through FOS. In fact, over 50 percent of all complaints referred to FOS are resolved in favour of the customer. You can check out all the statistics, including the best and worst companies, at: www.ombudsman-complaints-data.org.uk.

But with all that said and done, if FOS doesn't find in your favour, either, then you should probably just take what the insurer is offering you. Don't waste your time and money suing in court—it's highly unlikely that you'll win. In fact, recently an insurer took a policyholder to court after FOS found in the policyholder's favour—the court reversed FOS's judgement and ordered the policyholder to repay what they'd been awarded from FOS!

GETTING YOUR MONEY

Finally, when all is said and done and most of your items have been replaced, you'll probably be left waiting for some cash, too. There isn't actually a limit on the time that insurers can take to get you your cash. The rules just say that they have to settle the claim within a reasonable time period. Usually that will be within a week or two. Insurers have a few internal processes with some checks and balances, depending on the size of the cash settlement. That settlement will come in the form of a cheque made out to you or, more often these days, an electronic bank transfer.

If for some reason you want to assign the proceeds to someone else, you must first get prior agreement from the insurance company and they'll need explicit agreement from you, usually in the form of a letter, that you have agreed to this.

But once that money hits your bank account, you're golden. You're done. You saw it through to the end and got the result you wanted. Congratulations. It's time to start living your life again.

CHAPTER 8 RECAP

- **The offer you get from your insurer shouldn't be a surprise.**
- **If it seems low, ask them to demonstrate how they arrived at that value.**
- **You are the arbiter of whether or not an item has successfully been replaced.**
- **If you're really not happy, make a formal complaint (and refer it to FOS if you're still not happy after eight weeks).**

Conclusion

I've been in insurance for almost 30 years, almost since I left school. I've seen people literally standing in the ruins of their home, wondering how their lives could ever get back to normal. When you see a situation like that, you want to do whatever you can to help them.

That's how I got into starting my own business. I remember about 15 years ago I was called up to a tiny village up north. There were about 100 houses in this village, all of which were flooded up to the first floor level thanks to a cockup from the local authority. Most of the residents were pensioners with little or no insurance who had suddenly suffered this terrible event and literally didn't know what to do next. I was called up by the parish council to go there for a couple of days, talk to some of these people, and give them advice about how to deal with the situation. Those who were insured needed advice on how to handle their claims and those who weren't insured were potentially in line to get some money from the local authority as part of a relief fund so they needed some advice on how to spend that money if they ever got any. I was in a parish hall with people from 99 of those 100 houses, just talking to them about what was next, what they needed to do, and what they should be thinking about.

Afterwards the head of the council came up to me and said, "Joel, sorry about this, but Mrs Smith wasn't able to get out of her house today. Can you pop down the road to see her and talk to her?"

I thought about it and wondered whether I was being an ambulance chaser—whether I was cold-calling and exploiting this poor old woman's misery for profit. Then I asked myself, "Will this woman be in a better or a worse position from talking to me?" If the answer was that she'd be worse off, then I shouldn't even be in this business. But if she'd be better off, then I'd be doing her a disservice if I didn't go and talk to her, even just for five minutes. I have a moral and a human obligation to give people the information they need at the time that they need it.

Gone are the days when an insurer would not make a drama out of a crisis. It is all about selling your policy cheaper rather than delivering on the service you expect when you bought the product. Just look at the rise of the aggregating websites such as gocompare.com and others like it. Yet as consumers we accept this and we don't actually demand change.

It is my passion and belief that you do not have to be a victim of the claims process. It is your claim to make and not the insurance company's to dictate.

"Your claim" means that the claim must meet your needs and those needs are not just financial but include emotional support; practical support; and genuine, honest advice giving you the power to make the right decisions for you and your family and your business when everything looks bleak. It is about standing up for what is right, not what is convenient. It is putting service before profit, albeit profit being unnecessarily contingent on making the changes in the world. It is about ensuring that policyholders' needs are respected and honoured by the insurance company rather than just seeing them as another policy number.

These changes are vital to impact how we see ourselves as individuals and knowing that we don't have to accept whatever the computer says or the man in the suit says is right or wrong, but rather, knowing that we are right and we are entitled to stand until we are seen, heard, and listened to.

That's why I wrote this book.

Appendix

GLOSSARY OF KEY INSURANCE TERMS

ADDENDUM
A document setting out agreed alterations to an insurance contract. (See also "Endorsement.")

ADDITIONAL PREMIUM
A further premium, payable by the insured as a result of policy amendment, that may have increased the risk or changed the policy conditions or sum insured.

ADJUSTER
The person who investigates and assesses claims on behalf of insurers (claims adjuster or loss adjuster).

AGGREGATE LIMIT OF INDEMNITY
The maximum amount an insurer will pay under a policy in respect of all accumulated claims arising within a specified period of insurance.

ALL RISKS
Term used to describe insurance against loss of or damage to property arising from any fortuitous cause except those that are specifically excluded.

AVERAGE
A clause in insurance policies whereby, in the event of under-insurance, the claim paid out by the insurer is restricted to the same proportion of the loss as the sum insured under the policy bears to the total value of the insured item.

CLAIMS
Injury or loss to the insured arising so as to cause liability to the insurer under a policy it has issued.

COMMON LAW
The common law consists of the ancient customs and usages of the land which have been recognised by the courts and given the force of law. It is in itself a complex system of law, both civil and criminal, although it is greatly modified and extended by statute law and equity. It is unwritten and has come down in the recorded judgements of judges who, for hundreds of years, have interpreted it.

CONCEALMENT
Deliberate suppression by a proposer for insurance of a

material fact relating to the risk, usually making the contract null and void.

COVER NOTE
A document issued to the insured confirming details of the insurance cover placed. Some cover notes are a legal requirement, e.g. motor.

DEDUCTIBLE
The specified amount a loss must exceed before a claim is payable. Only the amount which is in excess of the deductible is recoverable.

ENDORSEMENT
Documentary evidence of a change in the wording of or cover offered by an existing policy or qualification of wording if the policy is written on restricted terms. (See also "Addendum.")

EXCESS
The first portion of a loss or claim which is borne by the insured. An excess can be either voluntary to obtain premium benefit or imposed for underwriting reasons.

EXCLUSION
A provision in a policy that excludes the insurer's liability in certain circumstances or for specified types of loss.

EX-GRATIA PAYMENT
A payment made by an insurer to a policyholder where there is no legal liability to pay.

FIRST LOSS INSURANCE

Insurance where the sum insured is accepted to be less than the value of the property but the insurer undertakes to pay claims up to the sum insured, without application of average.

HAZARD

A physical or moral feature that introduces or increases the risk.

INCEPTION DATE

The date from which, under the terms of a policy, an insurer is deemed to be at risk.

INDEMNITY

A principle whereby the insurer seeks to place the insured in the same position after a loss as he occupied immediately before the loss (as far as possible).

INSURABLE INTEREST

For a contract of insurance to be valid, the policyholder must have an interest in the insured item that is recognised at law whereby he benefits from its safety, well being, or freedom from liability and would be prejudiced by its damage or the existence of liability. This is called the "insurable interest" and must exist at the time the policy is taken out and at the time of the loss.

INSURABLE VALUE

The value of the insurable interest which the insured has in the insured occurrence or event. It is the amount to be paid out by the insurer (assuming full insurance) in the event of total loss or destruction of the item insured.

FINANCIAL OMBUDSMAN SERVICE

A bureau established by major insurance companies to oversee the interests of policyholders whose complaints remain unsolved through normal company channels of communication. The service is available to all those holding personal cover with the insurers who have joined the scheme. The decision of the ombudsman is binding on the insurer, although the insured may appeal to the court if he so wishes.

INSURED

The person whose property is insured or in whose favour the policy is issued.

INSURER

An insurance company that, in return for a consideration (a premium), agrees to make good in a manner laid down in the policy any loss or damage suffered by the person paying the premium as a result of some accident or occurrence.

LAPSE

The non-renewal of a policy for any reason.

LIMIT

The insurer's maximum liability under an insurance, which may be expressed "per accident," "per event," "per occurrence," "per annum," etc.

LOSS

Another term for a claim.

LOSS ADJUSTER

Independent, qualified loss adjusters are used by insurers for their experience and expertise necessary to carry out detailed and, in some instances, prolonged investigations of complex and large losses. Although the adjuster's fees are invariably paid by the insurers, he is an impartial professional person and makes his judgement on the amount to be paid in settlement solely on the basis of established market practice. It is his task to negotiate a settlement which is within the terms of the policy and equitable to both insured and insurer. Should he himself not be an expert in a particular discipline which is necessary or desirable to pursue his negotiations, he will consult or employ such an expert.

LOSS ASSESSOR
A person who, in return for a fee (usually a percentage of the amount claimed), acts for the claimant in negotiating the claim.

MATERIAL FACT
Any fact which would influence the insurer in accepting or declining a risk or in fixing the premium or terms and conditions of the contract is material and must be disclosed by a proposer or by the insurer to the insured.

NEGLIGENCE
The omission to do something which a reasonable man guided by those considerations which ordinarily regulate the conduct of human affairs would do, or doing something which a prudent and reasonable man would not do. Gives rise to civil liability.

NEW-FOR-OLD
Where insurers agree to pay the cost of property lost or

destroyed without deduction for depreciation.

NO CLAIMS BONUS (OR DISCOUNT)
A rebate of premium given to an insured person by an insurer where no claims have been made by that insured.

NON-DISCLOSURE
The failure by the insured or his broker to disclose a material fact or circumstance to the underwriter before acceptance of the risk.

PERIL
A contingency, of fortuitous happening, which may be covered or excluded by a policy of insurance.

PERIOD OF RISK
The period during which the insurer can incur liability under the terms of the policy.

POLICY
A document detailing the terms and conditions applicable to an insurance contract and constituting legal evidence of the agreement to insure. It is issued by an insurer or his representative for the first period of risk. On renewal, a new policy may well not be issued, although the same conditions would apply and the current wording would be evidence by the renewal receipt.

POLICY HOLDER
The person in whose name the policy is issued. (See also "Insured" and "Assured.")

PREMIUM
The consideration paid for a contract of insurance.

REINSTATEMENT
Making good. Where insured property is damaged, it is usual for settlement to be effected through the payment of a sum of money, but a policy may give either the insured or insurer the option to restore or rebuild instead.

RISK
The peril insured against or an individual exposure.

SCHEDULE
The part of a policy containing information peculiar to that particular risk. The greater part of a policy is likely to be identical for all risks within a class of business covered by the same insurer.

STATEMENT OF FACT
An alternative to a completed proposal form. A statement provided by the insurer clarifying the basis on which insurance is accepted and what conditions apply.

SUM INSURED
The maximum amount payable in the event of a claim under contract of insurance.

THIRD PARTY
A person claiming against an insured. In insurance terminology, the first party is the insurer and the second party is the insured.

THIRD PARTY LIABILITY
Liability of the insured to persons who are not parties to the contract of insurance and are not employees of the insured.

UTMOST GOOD FAITH
Insurance contracts are contracts of utmost good faith (*uberrima fides*), which means that both parties to the contract have a duty to disclose, clearly and accurately, all material facts relating to the proposed insurance. Any breach of this duty by the proposer may entitle the insurer to repudiate liability.

WARRANTY
A very strict condition in a policy imposed by an insurer. A breach entitles the insurer to deny liability.

WEAR AND TEAR
This is the amount deducted from claims payments to allow for any depreciation in the property insured which is caused by its usage.

WITHOUT PREJUDICE
A term used in discussion and correspondence. Where there is a dispute or negotiations for a settlement and terms are offered "without prejudice," an offer so made or a letter so marked and subsequent correspondence cannot be admitted in evidence without the consent of both parties concerned.

ADDITIONAL RESOURCES

MORE INFORMATION ON POLICY TERMS, AND CHOOSING THE RIGHT POLICY

- abi.org.uk/insurance-and-savings/products/home-insurance
- moneyadviceservice.org.uk/en/articles/contents-insurance-get-the-right-policy-and-cover
- moneysavingexpert.com/insurance/home-insurance
- moneysupermarket.com/home-insurance/guides/

SEEKING FURTHER HELP IN THE EVENT OF A CLAIM

- therightclaim.com
- citizensadvice.org.uk
- victimsupport.org.uk

MORE INFORMATION ON COMPLAINTS AND REGULATIONS

- financial-ombudsman.org.uk
- fca.org.uk

RECORDING AND RECALLING YOUR CONTENTS

- dropbox.com
- onedrive.com
- facebook.com
- instagram.com

VALUATIONS FOR PROPERTY OR ITEMS

- rics.org.uk
- amazon.co.uk

INFORMATION ON FLOODING AND WEATHER CONDITIONS

- environment-agency.gov.uk/flood
- metoffice.gov.uk

About the Author

JOEL ZIMELSTERN is the founder of The Right Claim, a consulting firm offering independent expert insurance service to households and businesses.

With over 28 years of experience in the UK insurance business, Joel works to help his clients present successful claims by understanding their policies, managing their cases, negotiating with insurance companies.

Through his writing, Joel educates non-clients on how they can do the same.

64408294R00071

Made in the USA
Charleston, SC
01 December 2016